101 More

Questions & Answers
about

STANDARDS,
ASSESSMENT,
and
ACCOUNTABILITY

Advanced Learning Press
Denver, Colorado

Douglas B. Reeves, Ph

ISBN #0-9747343-0-6

Limited Reproduction Permission: Permission is hereby granted for individual teachers and educators to reproduce the forms for classroom use. Reproduction of these materials for an entire school system is strictly forbidden.

Advanced Learning Press books are available for quantity discounts with bulk purchases for education systems, professional organizations, or sales promotion use. For more details and discount information, contact Advanced Learning Press at (800) 844-6599 or fax (303) 504-9417.

Project editor: Allison W. Schumacher and Ken Bingenheimer

Printed and Bound in the United States of America

Published by:

Advanced Learning Press
317 Inverness Way South, Suite 150 • Englewood, CO 80112
(800) 844-6599 or (303) 504-9312 • fax (303) 504-9417
www.MakingStandardsWork.com

Reeves, Douglas B., 1953–
    101 more questions & answers about standards, assessment, and accountability / Douglas B. Reeves.
        p. cm.
    Includes bibliographical references and index.
    ISBN 0-9747343-0-6 (pbk.)
    1. Education--Standards--United States--Miscellanea. 2. Education--United States--Evaluation--Miscellanea. 3. Educational accountability--United States--Miscellanea. I. Title: One hundred one more questions and answers about standards, assessment, and accountability. II. Title: One hundred and one more questions and answers about standards, assessment, and accountability. III. Title: Title.

    LB3060.83.R44 2004
    379.1'58'0973--dc22   2004047648

About the Author

Dr. Douglas Reeves is chairman and founder of the Center for Performance Assessment, an international organization dedicated to improving student achievement and educational equity. Through its long-term relationships with school systems, the Center helps educators and school leaders to improve student achievement through practical and constructive approaches to standards, assessment, and accountability.

Dr. Reeves is a frequent keynote speaker in the U.S. and abroad for education, government, and business organizations and is a faculty member of leadership programs sponsored by the Harvard Graduate School of Education. The author of seventeen books and many articles, Doug is the author of the best-selling *Making Standards Work*, now in its third edition. Other recent titles include *Assessing Educational Leaders: Evaluating Performance for Improved Individual and Organizational Results* (Corwin Press, 2004), *Accountability for Learning: How Teachers and School Leaders Can Take Charge* (ASCD, 2004), *The Daily Disciplines of Leadership: How to Improve Student Achievement, Staff Morale, and Personal Organization* (Jossey-Bass, 2002), *The Leader's Guide to Standards: A Blueprint for Educational Excellence and Equity* (Jossey-Bass, 2002), and *Reason to Write: Help Your Child Succeed in School and In Life Through Better Reasoning and Clear Communication* (Simon & Schuster, 2002). Doug has twice been selected for the Harvard Distinguished Authors Series and he recently won the Parents' Choice Award for his writing for children and parents.

Beyond his work in large-scale assessment and research, Doug has devoted many years to classroom teaching with students ranging from elementary school to doctoral candidates. Doug's family includes four children ranging from elementary school through college, all of whom have attended public schools. His wife, Shelley Sackett, is an attorney, mediator, and school board member. He lives near Boston and can be reached at dreeves@MakingStandardsWork.com.

Contents

Introduction

In the three years since the publication of the first volume of *101 Questions & Answers about Standards, Assessment, and Accountability*, Dr. Reeves and the Center for Performance Assessment have continued to receive and respond to real-world questions from teachers, school leaders, parents, students, and educational researchers. Now, in the age of increased accountability and No Child Left Behind, Dr. Reeves offers this second collection of questions and answers that addresses a new set of issues affecting education today. Topics include:

- Establishing Power Standards for elective courses

- Evaluating the benefits of teaching to prescribed standards and developing building- or district-specific Power Standards

- Aligning leaders' approaches to standards-based instruction and accountability

- Preparing students for university acceptance based on norm-referenced versus criterion-referenced scoring

- Collecting data from both district-wide and building-wide assessments

- Measuring student achievement in reading and writing

- Evaluating achievement for ESL, remedial, and gifted students

Together with the first collection of questions and answers, this second volume will help all stakeholders in education today formulate effective solutions and improve communication within the school community.

Power
Standards

Power Standards

1   **We have been working with the concept of Power Standards in our district, and the following questions have come up: What are the differences between Power Standards, essential learnings, common outcomes, viable curriculum, learning targets, etc.? Or are they different ways of stating and answering the question, 'What are the core things we want all kids to learn as a result of instruction?'**

 You have identified one of the most vexing parts of every curriculum discussion: We use different words to mean the same thing, and the same words to mean different things. I would settle for this language: "What students must know and be able to do." That's it. I could use that in discussing this issue with teachers, professors, or 3rd graders. This is particularly important in the context of Power Standards, because they are, by definition, a much smaller subset of the complete list of things that are found in the typical list of "learnings, outcomes, results, standards, indicators, objectives, benchmarks, etc." What all of those things have in common is that they are TOO LONG and, as a result, are never a realistic list of what students must know and be able to do. Power Standards, by contrast, apply three filters to the long lists. Those filters are endurance, leverage, and necessity for the next level of instruction. For an excellent discussion of this, please see Larry Ainsworth's books entitled *Power Standards* and *"Unwrapping" the Standards*.

2   **Could you relate to me your basic philosophy behind the credibility of standards if they do not measure spurious relationships with variables such as learning disabilities phenomena and test anxiety? Is it even possible? How do policymakers reconcile this dilemma?**

First, we must separate the issue of standards from standardized testing. There are many instances in which the standards—clear expressions of what students should know and be able to do—are fine, but the standardized tests that purport to measure the achievement of those standards are deeply flawed.

Second, in the cases of learning disabilities, it is a matter of federal law (the Individuals with Disabilities Education Act—IDEA) that the civil rights of these students are protected. Specifically, they have the right to appropriate accommodations and adaptations in curriculum and testing. In the cases of physical disabilities, these are rather straightforward: Blind students can have readers, students without motor function can have writers, etc. In the cases of the far more common learning disabilities, however, the adaptations are more inconsistent. In most cases, extra time is provided, but this may not be a sufficient adaptation depending on the needs of the students. The key thing to remember here is that it is not the fault of the standards when the adaptations are inappropriate; it is rather the fault of inadequate consideration of the needs of the individual student. We do students with learning disabilities, test anxiety, or any other challenge no favors when we say, "Gee, they just can't meet the standard, so forget about it." This is particularly pernicious when a disproportionate number of poor and minority children are classified as learning disabled. Rather, what we must do is to maintain the standards, but create ways for every student to have an appropriate opportunity to meet those standards, and that implies much more care to the individual needs of students. To summarize: standards, yes; standardization, no.

3 **What do administrators and state department officials emphasize most: coverage of everything in the textbook or academic performance as measured on state tests?**

If the answer is the latter—and I know of nowhere in the country where that is not the case—then the issue is results. If a school were to use Power Standards or any other technique and fail to improve student performance, then administrators and state department officials would be unhappy. If a school uses Power Standards and student performance improves, then administrators and state department officials are delighted. Therefore, the only question is this: Do Power Standards improve academic performance? In fact, we have already developed case studies around the nation that prove the obvious: Focus on key academic subjects is effective. But no one at the Center for Performance Assessment has ever asserted that Power Standards alone are the cause of improved student achievement. This is one technique among many that is necessary for improved achievement. Schools that only use Power Standards, but fail to reallocate the way that they spend time, score student work collaboratively, and dramatically increase nonfiction writing with editing and rewriting should not expect much improvement. What Power Standards allow the classroom teacher to do is FOCUS—dispensing with the illusion that frantic coverage is equivalent to student learning. With focus comes time for more literacy instruction, student feedback, and teacher collaboration. Schools that implement an entire complement of ideas to improve academic achievement, and then monitor that implementation every week at the classroom level, will see improved results.

4   We are trying to make sure that there are no loopholes in our policies as we implement our standards-based system. Can you direct me to a district that has 'teaching to standards as a non-negotiable' in its board/district governing policies?

The only instance I'm aware of in which teaching to standards was potentially NOT part of contractual expectations was the recent California attempt to make curriculum and standards a matter of local negotiation. That proposal failed in the state assembly, no doubt because both federal and state laws include requirements for the use of academic content standards.

Otherwise, it's not necessary to stipulate that "teachers must teach to standards" when the contract (and state laws) already include provisions for the local school board specifying the terms of curriculum and instruction. For teachers to suggest otherwise is no different that someone saying that the school board and administrators cannot determine the start of the work day, the adherence to safety instructions, or the relationships between teachers and students. The myth that "academic freedom" means that teachers can do whatever they want to do is simply that—a myth—and it is not an exemption from state and federal law.

My recommendation is that you not let this become a contract issue. The district already has authority over curriculum and instruction, and to raise the issue only suggests that matters of equity and equal opportunity for education are negotiable.

5   **How do you implement standards without spending hours working on plans? Can you recommend some resources on this subject?**

You're right that implementation can sometimes be impeded, rather than helped, by endless plans and processes. For some quick guidelines to get started, see the "Standards Implementation Checklist" that is in the book *Making Standards Work*. In addition, The *Leader's Guide to Standards* should be helpful here. Another resource you should consider is the *Video Journal of Education*, Volumes 802 and 803. It provides footage of teachers implementing standards at the classroom level, and is much more compelling than just having people listening to a lecture about standards. Please consult the list of references at the back of this book for more information.

6   As we work with the idea of Power Standards, I hear teachers express the concern that there are parts of the content that need to be introduced and explored at a grade level in order for the students to meet the Power Standards at the next grade level. These introduced and explored areas don't seem to be coming through in the Power Standards, yet are necessary for student success over time. Are we missing something in the process of determining Power Standards or in the interpretation of the intent?

This is the very issue that leads to excessive quantities of stuff for which no one takes responsibility because, after all, this is just "introduction" or "exposure." Power Standards represent ONLY those areas where students WILL become proficient, not merely exposed. That is why it is important to have a small number of Power Standards: Leaders and students must ensure that Power Standards are learned by students, not merely delivered so that students can be exposed to them. It is fine if teachers want to have an idea of some introductory concepts for context, but we must be very, very clear about priorities. When time is short in the classroom—and it almost always is—and teachers have to make a choice between two competing curriculum options, it is always better to devote energy to student success and proficiency NOW rather than exposure and introduction to things that will not lead to proficiency.

7   Some teachers claim that universities will never stand for a standards-based education approach because they need GPAs, class ranks, valedictorians, etc. We already know of the PASS program in Oregon, but are there any other examples of universities preferring or allowing the SBE approach?

I'm not advocating the elimination of grades. I recognize that they are part of our cultural landscape. However, a lot of schools—not just in Oregon—are looking at portfolios, community service, multiple scores, etc. Society wants grades, and we will give them grades. Nevertheless, we can also give parents and students standards achievement reports, showing clearly which standards students meet and which standards they do not meet. For elaboration, see the December 2000 issue of the National Association of Secondary Schools Principals *Bulletin*, where Guskey, Marzano, and I have offered ideas on how to do this.

8   **What is the balance between asking a district to start from scratch in identifying standards and creating assessments, and handing the district a "best of" list of standards and assessments? I understand that the collaborative efforts of a district's staff will gain greater buy-in as well as an increased level of sustainability, but it strikes me that there would be some standards that have proven to be "timeless" and "borderless."**

Your instincts on collaboration are right. Even if it might be obvious, you still want collaboration. When Power Standards are announced, it's far better for the district to say, "based on the work done at the building level, 90 percent of teachers agree that these really are Power Standards" rather than "we are the curriculum experts around here and we know what's best for you."

9   **I've been asked by my district to help create Power Standards for the visual arts. My dilemma is that there are only five visual arts content standards. Are Power Standards really necessary if there are only five standards to begin with and the five standards are pretty clear?**

I understand your concern about the initially small number of standards. Nevertheless, the essence of Power Standards is the understanding that not every standard is equally important for students to enter the next grade level with success and confidence. Moreover, time and resources are limited, so teachers and parents must have a better set of guidelines than to "cover every standard." The use of Power Standards does not prevent a teacher in ideal circumstances from addressing every standard, but it does provide clear guidance when the ideal circumstances are not available. Reasonable people can differ on this point, and of course I defer to your district on this matter. But my candid advice is that Power Standards are necessary, and the failure to use them allows us to engage in the fantasy that everything will be covered and learned. One special note: The very fact that your district included the visual arts in its discussion of standards is OUTSTANDING. The vast majority of districts totally ignore that area in their standards discussions.

10 I believe our 'standards' are actually 'do' lists and so complicated, long, and repetitive that they scare teachers away. Is there an example available of what 'Power Standards' might look like and what benchmarks might be at a particular grade level?

Part of the problem is terminology. What one state calls "standards," another state calls "indicators," "benchmarks," or "core curriculum." I'd suggest returning to a more basic level of English expression: What students are expected to know and be able to do. If we articulate those requirements, then we have taken the first step toward successful standards implementation. Using that plain-language definition, I do believe that you can substantially narrow the focus of what we expect of students to six to twelve items per grade level per subject. This is in marked contrast to the eighty-six standards for Ohio 6th graders in math, or the ninety standards for California 9th graders in English. Whether you call it a benchmark, standard, or other term, there are too many of them in every state. Therefore, the obligation of teachers and leaders at the school level is to add value to state standards with prioritization and focus.

This "value-added" process implies that teachers and leaders make some necessary choices, deciding to exclude certain state standards. This is not—I checked—a felony. In fact, every teacher in the nation excludes some standards, but most of them make this exclusion by default, deciding in the last few weeks of the school year the standards that they will not have time to achieve. A far better process is to decide NOW—at the beginning of the year—what standards are the most important and which ones can be consigned to the scrap heap. Covering everything is not an option; it's a fantasy in which only state department people who do not associate with children or teachers can engage. For the rest of us, we can choose only two paths: coverage by design or coverage by default. I favor the former course.

11 **You specifically talked about cutting the 6th grade math standards from over eighty down to seven essential standards. Have you done this with all subjects in all grade levels? If you have, is this information published somewhere and how can we get it? What were the seven standards for the 6th grade math program? We have teachers doing report cards by going through a check-off system of every standard a child has met. So far, this has only affected the elementary level, but the middle school is next for the same process. I'm a special education teacher and I know how paperwork takes away from the time it takes to prepare to teach. There has to be a better way.**

We have provided some examples of Power Standards, but they are only for illustration purposes. There is no substitute for your OWN faculty members going through your standards and asking:

1. What endures?

2. What has leverage?

3. What is really necessary for success at the next grade level?

Then, of course, the job is not done. The next step is to agree on common assessments that all faculty members will use so that the focus on these Power Standards has meaning and consistency.

New York tried to do a report card including every standard, and it took them twelve pages for 4th graders. That has, thankfully, been abandoned. It just alienates parents and teachers alike. What is quite reasonable, however, is to have the report card reflect seven to ten standards that are absolutely vital for future success. In that way, even if a student gets (through the alchemy of the grading process) a C or a B, the parents will still know if the student is not succeeding in critical areas.

You can find some examples of language arts standards in the book *Reason to Write* (Simon & Schuster, 2002).

You asked for the 6th grade math Power Standards. They are:

1. Number operations with and without a calculator.

2. Tables, charts, graphs: Create them given a data set and draw inferences from them once they are completed.

3. Fraction and decimal operations: again, with and without a calculator.

4. Measurement in English and metric units.

5. Given a story problem, convert it to an accurate picture.

6. Properties of a triangle and rectangle.

7. Two-dimensional scale drawing.

I'm fully aware that there are many other things in the 6th grade curriculum, but every 7th and 8th grade teacher I've ever interviewed has said they would be happier if students could do these seven things rather than be "checked off" on eighty other things that are in the standards.

Show Me the Proof

 12 I am trying to answer staff questions regarding the Power Standards we heard you speak about. I believe you stated there are six Power Standards that have twenty-five years worth of research. Can you assist in the efforts of locating these identified Power Standards?

 It's a relatively new concept, so I must have used the "twenty-five years of research" in a different context. Here is what we do know:

1. There are many decades of research about the relationship between writing and student achievement, about the impact of teacher quality on student achievement, and about the ability of poor and minority students to succeed. The reference list at the back of this or any other book I have written (as well as many free downloads from our web site, www.MakingStandardsWork.com) will attest to this.

2. Power Standards are a simple acknowledgment of the truth: There are too many standards and not enough time to cover them all. We can either have "coverage by default"—deciding what not to do in June after we run out of time—or "coverage by design"—deciding what to do based on its importance.

3. The process of selecting Power Standards is straightforward and best described in two books by my colleague, Larry Ainsworth. The books are *Power Standards* and *"Unwrapping" the Standards*.

13 Can you recommend some resources to help me convince my colleagues that it is better to measure students against a standard than against each other? I am trying to show them that standards-based education is our best option to improve student achievement, but they are demanding proof.

The term "standards-based" is so broad and the variables in education so many, that no one can make a credible case that any individual process is the causal variable that determines student achievement. Nevertheless, we can definitely support the following contentions.

When standards (as opposed to student-to-student comparisons) are used to evaluate student achievement, and when these standards are linked to classroom instruction, and when these standards are clear, rigorous, and consistent:

1. Student achievement improves.

2. Research supporting the impact of standards is cross-cultural, including studies about Europeans, Africans, and North Americans.

3. It is not the establishment of standards, but their implementation that is the principal leadership and teaching variable. Thus a state can have standards, with some schools failing while others are succeeding. It is the degree of implementation, not the mere existence of standards, that matters.

4. Even if there were not a particle of statistical evidence supporting standards, it is a fact that standards are fairer than the alternative—the bell curve. Fairness stands alone as a sufficient justification for the standards-based approach to education.

5. Support for standards-based education comes from a wide spectrum of political views, from conservative to liberal.

I'll be happy to suggest reference lists to support these contentions, but it would be helpful to know the audience. A brief list includes:

- The Education Trust—www.edtrust.org—specifically, check the download "Dispelling the Myth, Revisited."

- Linda Darling-Hammond—specifically, check the first 100 pages or so of *The Right to Learn*.

- E.D. Hirsch, *The Schools We Need*—specifically, check his international references to the impact of standards-based education on African immigrants in France.

- Reeves, D.B., *The Leader's Guide to Standards*—specifically check the early chapter on "Why Standards?".

14 **I remember that you mentioned a study that showed pretty convincingly that teachers who were faced with 'mile wide, inch deep' curriculum could actually raise scores on tests designed to test coverage of the curriculum by focusing on the main concepts and teaching them well. This was one of the main points behind the 'Power Standards' concept. I would like a reference to this study if I can get one. I want to be able to actually quote it rather than just sharing hearsay.**

The most important research on this comes from the third Trends in International Math and Science Study, all of which can be downloaded for free at http://isc.bc.edu/timss2003.html." Essentially, you will see that there is an inverse relationship between the number of standards addressed and the success of the students. Japan, Germany, Korea, and Singapore have about 1/7th the number of subjects in math and science that our students must cover. Yet on the same test, they do much better. This is hardly a function of international tests. We work with districts that have greatly reduced the science curriculum, focusing on a few standards doing elementary science once a week, and devoting the remainder of the time to literacy enhancement. Their science scores have more than doubled.

For additional independent reviews of the impact of more focused curriculum, see the National Science Foundation's study called the Valle Imperial Project in Science (or VIPS). It is published under the title "Helping English Learners Increase Achievement Through Inquiry-Based Science Instruction" in the Summer 2002 edition of the *Bilingual Research Journal* and is available for free download at http://brj.asu.edu.

Two additional resources for more information are Linda Darling-Hammond's wonderful book, *The Right to Learn*, which addresses this in the first 100 pages, and James Hiebert and Jim Stigler's *The Teaching Gap*. Finally, see my books *Accountability in Action: A Blueprint for Learning Organizations* (see the chapter on Power Standards) and, from Jossey-Bass, *The Leader's Guide to Standards*.

Standards-Based Performance Assessment

15 I understand that you are in favor of standardized testing but not the bell curve as a comparative evaluation because of the diversity within. What other means of measurement can we use? As a future administrator, what more can I do?

 The only measurement I find useful and fair is the comparison of students to a standard, not the comparison of students to each other. In other words, if I want my students to be proficient in analytical writing, I don't want to know, "Are my kids better than kids in Kansas City?" but rather "Are my students able to analyze the similarities and differences in two topics, create an appropriate graphic organizer or outline to display those differences, create a rough draft of an analytical essay, engage in self-editing and peer-editing to improve that rough draft, and then create a final draft that is suitable for publication?" In a shorter question, "Can my students meet the standard?" That is the essence of a standards-based assessment rather than a norm-referenced assessment.

I don't know if I'm improving with age, but perhaps some of my books are. See if the library has copies of *The Leader's Guide to Standards* and *The Daily Disciplines of Leadership*. These volumes might do a better job of encouraging a future administrator to use academic standards as a vehicle to improve student achievement and educational equity.

16 Should I ask my teachers to set measurable goals for each quarter? My hunch is that this would be micro-managing and that they should give assessments with their annual goals in mind, look at the results, celebrate gains in proficiency, and focus on the areas that are causing the most difficulty in the next nine-week period. But I thought I should ask the master. What do you recommend?

I'm more convinced that the measurement itself is what's necessary. If the year-end goal is clear—say, 100 percent of students scoring "proficient" or higher on a collaboratively scored nonfiction writing prompt—then it doesn't make any difference whether the progress is linear or nonlinear. Rather, the issue is that they measure their progress and agree on the destination, and, most importantly, that they are talking in December about how January will be different, based on the measurements they have done so far. I'm convinced that a lot of central office (and external consultant) cross-examinations and surveys could be replaced by one question: How will next quarter be different from last quarter based on what you now know about student achievement in your school?

This is a long-winded way of saying that I agree with you. Quarterly goals are not nearly as important as quarterly midcourse corrections to achieve the annual goal.

17 **We want all of our administrators to have the same understanding of what we mean when we talk about common assessment. Could you give us some recommended readings that we could provide to all of our administrators to give us all a common knowledge base regarding common assessment?**

Let me offer these ideas:

Why? Common assessments have been associated with schools in holistic accountability studies that have had significantly higher performance in language arts, math, science, and social studies than schools that are demographically similar, but do not use common assessments.

What? Common assessments do not represent daily micromanagement of the curriculum, but the recognition that at periodic intervals we should have common expectations of students. Those common expectations are frequently expressed in standards and curriculum documents and sometimes expressed in lesson plans. But none of those documents is as precise in interpreting what real expectations by teachers of students are in practice as the common assessment. At the high school level, this means a common final exam, administered at the end of each semester. At the middle school level, it implies end-of-quarter assessments. At the elementary level, it means common monthly assessments.

Common assessments are NOT used for every standard and every class. Rather, educators and administrators look at their data and consider what their greatest needs are. They consider which subjects have the greatest leverage over other subjects. It might be sufficient, depending on the data analysis, for a school to only have common assessments at the high school level in core academic subjects and at the middle and elementary school level in reading comprehension, nonfiction writing, and math problem solving.

Flexibility: I know of districts that imposed a common assessment program, but gave individual schools the opportunity to be exempt from the district common assessment system if the school could demonstrate to the district that it already had in place a program of common assessments that met the district objectives.

How? Ideally, the district first establishes its "Power Standards"—that subset of standards that are most important for long-term student success. The common assessments do not address every standard, but rather only the Power Standards. This leaves plenty of room for classroom assessment that can vary from one teacher to another, depending on the needs of students and the emphasis of that teacher. But on the most important standards, there is consistency among all educators.

Is this a great deal of extra work? You should start by asking the question, "Are we assessing students using the state standards right now?" If so, the evidence of that will provide the basis for new assessments. If there are uniform claims that standards-based assessments are taking place, but few examples are produced, then the district must confront the fact that there is a gap, at least in some cases, between the claim to be "standards-based" and the classroom reality.

More details: For a terrific example of implementation of common assessments, consider the Palm Springs Unified School District. Working with Eileen Allison, the district created Power Standards and common assessments. Norfolk Public Schools have done similar work, as have schools in Indianapolis in the Wayne Township system.

18 What four steps characterize performance assessment and what happens at each step?

You've asked a very specific question that suggests you are referring to something you've read or seen or heard stating that there are specifically four steps that characterize performance assessment. Not knowing to what you are referring, it is hard to answer directly.

Four key steps in the Center's model of performance assessment would include:

1. Identify the primary standard.

2. Develop an engaging scenario.

3. Develop requirements for students to apply, analyze, and demonstrate knowledge.

4. Develop scoring guides (rubrics).

The first step addresses the question, "If I were to place this completed assignment in a student's portfolio, for which standards would it demonstrate proficiency?"

The second involves devising a real-world problem for the student to address that requires him or her to demonstrate proficiency. An example would be, in a chemistry class, to pose the question "Is the water safe to drink?" The third step would then be to turn the student loose to determine how that would be accomplished.

Finally, scoring guides are created in advance, with examples of work that is exemplary, proficient, progressing, and not meeting the standard. These clearly show the student what is expected of them and what they need to do to demonstrate proficiency on the assignment.

All this and much more can be found in my book, *Making Standards Work*. There are also sample performance assessments that you can download from our website, www.MakingStandardsWork.com. Teacher-created performance assessments, samples created by the Center, and an "unwrapped, standards-based performance assessment template," can be downloaded from our Resource Center on the site.

19   I have heard of research supporting the value of 'dramatic representations' performed by students to demonstrate what they've learned. Is it possible for you to let me know whose research this is?

The source is *Classroom Instruction That Works* by Robert Marzano and Debra Pickering, published by ASCD. In particular, they focus on one of their nine essential strategies being different representations of the same idea, and the examples of this include graphic organizers, dramatic representations, visual displays, and other alternative ways of expressing understanding.

One mistake that teachers frequently make is that, with the best of intentions, they give students many choices of how to present information. Some do story boards, some build models, some do papers, while others do oral presentations. In fact, each student must get more opportunities to represent the SAME ideas in a VARIETY of different ways. Consider this simple example:

In my math class, I want students to express mathematical ideas in three different ways:

1. Symbolically—A = LxW

2. Verbally—The area of a rectangle is the product of its length and width

3. Numerically—For the rectangle of the football field, the area is 100 yards multiplied by 40 yards, or 4000 square yards.

From this simple example, multiple other examples could spring, using graphs, charts, dramatic presentations, three-dimensional images, interactive computer games, etc. The whole idea is take a SINGLE idea, from the area of a rectangle to the causes of the American Revolution, and express it in many different ways.

20 **I am looking for a measure that is reliable, fair, and helpful for accountability. I have heard of an entrance and exit exam or evaluation for middle school students specifically. Can you suggest anything?**

For middle schools, I would offer not a single answer, but a combination of measurements.

First, consider the establishment of middle school "Power Standards." You can download an example of these for free at our website, www.MakingStandardsWork.com. I've also written about the concept of Power Standards in the book *Accountability in Action: A Blueprint for Learning Organizations*.

Second, hold a joint meeting between the high school and middle school faculty with the explicit objective of answering this question: What are the knowledge and skills that a student needs in order to enter high school with success and confidence? I suspect that you will identify not only information about content knowledge and literacy, but also about time management, organization, teamwork, and behavior—all elements that should figure prominently in your middle school Power Standards.

Third, consider a combined internal and external assessment. If you will have some students leave your system and attend other high schools, then an internationally accepted benchmark such as the SSAT (Secondary School Admissions Test) or ISEE (Independent School Entrance Examination) might be appropriate. In addition, consider establishing a portfolio for each student that demonstrates the achievement of high standards in writing (descriptive, analytical, and persuasive), mathematics (a mathematical model, including illustration with graphs and a few explanatory paragraphs), science (a completed lab report), social studies (an explanation of a historical event that integrates history, geography, and culture), and some elective entry that would reflect the unique characteristics of your school and the unique talents of that student. The latter could be a computer program, video, poem, religious/cultural analysis, or whatever you believe to be appropriate. The advantage of such a portfolio is that bad entries can be replaced by good ones and students can become accustomed to describing the difference between great work, adequate work, and unsatisfactory work.

21 Last year I established benchmarks for each administration of an assessment and measured the percentage of students who met the benchmark. The benchmark changed for each administration of assessment; that is, the mid-year benchmark was 50 percent, while the March benchmark was 70 percent.

We then measured the percentage of students in each class that met the benchmark.

Would it be more "valid" to use a 70 percent benchmark for each administration of the tests or would a changing benchmark be better? I found that setting a benchmark was very valuable in monitoring progress, however, in some cases the mid-year "pass rate" per class was considerably higher than the March pass rate (with a higher benchmark.) I wonder if teachers became complacent when the mid-year rate was relatively high, which resulted in a lower "pass rate" in March.

I think that the staff and students are best served by consistency. This would imply, of course, a lower pass rate in the early months, but with good progress and focus, it gives you a "stair-step" chart that shows continuous progress over the year. If you change the content or change the benchmark, then, as you suggest, the chart declines at the end of the year. Our purpose is to show them in the fall that they have work to do, and then in the spring, to show them that their hard work paid off.

22 We have teachers working on common, frequent curricular assessments to determine student levels of proficiency on identifed "Power Standards" in each grade level and content area. Our next phase will be to begin to develop performance assessments that can provide data that can replace some of these common curricular assessments and to develop a standards-based reporting system for parents.

We have provided the teachers with a suggested assessment format that will ensure that all levels of Bloom's *Taxonomy* are assessed.

Suggested Assessment Format:

- One question on an explanation of their learning
- 2-3 multiple choice
- 2-3 true/false, where the student must underline the part that makes the statement true, and if false, correct it
- One application or scenario problem

Can you give me feedback on this format? In particular, I have a question on the development of the scoring guide that will accompany the assessment. Do you have a recommendation on how teachers should evaluate multiple items on an assessment to determine a student's level of proficiency?

First, congratulations to you and your colleagues for using Power Standards and common assessments. These are some of the most effective strategies to improve achievement and equity in any school.

With regard to your questions on format, I endorse your idea of short, focused assessments, with a small number of multiple choice and performance questions. I would counsel against "true/false" questions because they only provide "binary" feedback: The students know it or they don't. Both multiple choice and performance items, by contrast, can help teachers know what students DO know, as well as which distracters students choose (in the case of multiple choice items) and what students use as reasoning patterns (in the case of performance items).

With regard to your question on the scoring rubrics, my advice is that each separate task should have its own rubric, rather than a holistic rubric for a multitask assessment. The reason for this is that the more specific the rubric, the better the feedback for students and teachers. I am also an advocate of four-point rubrics, including exemplary, proficient, progressing, and not meeting standards. The "exemplary" level should be FAR above the work required to be proficient, and should challenge your most advanced students. "Exemplary" is not only quantitatively more work, but QUALITATIVELY different in reasoning, sophistication, research, public display, and multiple representations of ideas. To see an example of what I mean for such multitask performance assessments, please see the appendices to my book, *Making Standards Work*, and in particular the "Ideal School" assessment.

23 **Our administration requires us to assess our students weekly and compare their progress to a pacing chart that they have provided for us. Not only do we find it difficult to keep up, but I feel that we are missing out on the bigger picture of actually analyzing our students' true strengths and weaknesses. Do you have any insights?**

Giving weekly tests and following the pacing chart are not enough if teachers do not do as you suggest—"analyze my students' true strengths and weaknesses." When I'm asked how this applies to daily teaching practice, the first thing I usually suggest is that we stand in a cold shower and tear our lesson plans into small pieces. That doesn't mean lesson plans are a bad idea, but it does mean that a pacing chart telling me to teach my 6th grade students all about exponents has little value if they cannot remember how to multiply. The same happens all the time when the essential foundations of learning are presumed by a curriculum document, and the real world of the classroom makes that assumption inaccurate.

So, what to do with the bureaucracy pulling one way and the real needs of students pulling the other? Some practical ideas:

Never, ever give one-shot assessments. If a concept is worth assessing, it's worth using that assessment to provide feedback for students and teachers, and then reassessing to see if your revised instruction was effective. That means every writing assessment ALWAYS has a rewrite. Even a multiple choice assessment that has a score of less that 80 percent (I know of teachers who say less than 95 percent, and that's in poor and minority schools!) requires a retake. They know that standards are not about speed, but about proficiency. Students have become too accustomed to doing a lot of work poorly and quickly. Slow down, get proficient, and do it as many times as you need. When you think about it, that's precisely what kids do on the basketball court or when holding an electronic game. I also remind people that the "standard" for Nintendo or basketball never changes based on the ethnicity or income of the player. It's completely consistent, and kids get very, very good at those games.

Employ Power Standards. I don't know if you've read Larry Ainsworth's book on that subject. There are also chapters in *Reason to Write* and in *Accountability in Action* on Power Standards. The concept is what every teacher knows: There are too many standards and somebody has to distinguish clearly between those that require mere coverage and those that require proficiency by students. Coverage and proficiency are not at all the same things, and the emphasis on pacing charts is usually only about coverage.

Use every second of the school day, including music, art, PE, technology, world languages, etc. to support academic content standards. We have collected many wonderful examples of this. It moves those subjects from the "it's not tested so it's not important" category to a genuine contribution for all faculty members.

Change the bloody schedule. There is just no substitute. If 40 percent of my kids in 5th grade are reading below grade level, then somebody needs to figure out that they spent 10 years getting into this mess and they won't get out of it in summer school. They need more time—lots of it—in literacy. In the most successful schools we study, they devote three hours a day to literacy—two in reading and one in writing, without fail, every single day. This is just too revolutionary for a lot of people who have not changed a schedule for decades to imagine.

24 **In the process of implementing standards-based education in our high school, we are encountering considerable resistance from teachers regarding relearning and reassessing in the classroom for students who did not achieve proficiency in the initial assessment. We hear all the usual reasons from "it makes my class too easy," to "there is no retaking in real life," and all the other usual excuses. What can I say to them?**

Please ask your colleagues to consider what "real life" requires. Is the feedback model of the world's most successful enterprises, "Here it is, boss. First draft, take it or leave it," or is the feedback model, "Here is it is, listen to and respect feedback, improve it, here it is again, listen to and respect feedback again, improve it . . ."? If it is the latter, the improvement cycle continues. The description of the "real world" as one-shot assessment is a description of the 19th century, not the 21st. One-shot assessment describes how students come into class, not how their performance is improved by listening to and respecting teacher feedback. I might add parenthetically that on the things that society really values—football, for instance—the teachers never use one-shot feedback, but use their "classes" to give students the opportunity to try techniques again, again, and again until they are perfected. They also don't use the average, but evaluate their season based on proficiency at the end, not the beginning. Why to we find that concept elusive in academic classes?

25   Does a district-wide assessment destroy building-based work?

On the contrary, building-based assessment is the proper START to this, but not the END. You start by allowing each school to find its own Power Standards and common assessments, and then see if all expectations are comparable. If they are, then copy them off, share them with other schools, and you have a wonderful database of test items. But in the other 99.9 percent of school districts, you will find that some schools expect more and others expect less. Do not just look at the assessments. Look at the assessments AND examples of student work that each school regards as proficient. Then remove any identifying information on the test and student work so that you won't know which school or which student has completed the work. Are all of these expectations really comparable or not?

The good news is that you will be able to honor school-based teacher work by finding common requirements among all schools. By identifying these common expectations, you will avoid the charge of a "top-down" initiative. You can say, "This district assessment represents the consensus of 80 percent of our teachers." But you will also find wide differences in student work that is regarded as "proficient," and this is the issue that must be confronted. You may get a lot of resistance to sending copies of student work that has been marked C or B, even if you assured privacy and anonymity for the students. The plain truth is that C and B work is MUCH different in schools based on widely varying expectations.

My fundamental conclusion is this: You do not have standards unless you have a professional consensus among buildings and among teachers on what the word "proficient" means. If you are not willing to say that every 9th grade student, regardless of neighborhood, is expected to know and do the same things, than you do not have standards, but an institutionalized bell curve.

26 I am struggling to find a way to assess my students on what they know while helping them achieve more on the state test. Should I give them a multiple choice assessment (because the state test is multiple choice) on capitalization if that is all that has been covered? That way, I would have a better understanding of where the student needs help before proceeding to the next topic. But the other issue is what will help the students score higher on the state mandated test. I believe that this method would assess where students are at that point in the curriculum, it would assess where teachers may need help, and it would give the superintendent a better idea whether the students are 'on target' with the curriculum.

Here is another potential compromise: Have the multiple choice items more narrowly focused, as you suggest, but also include performance items that would encompass potential student achievement on many additional standards, including those that have not been taught. In the example you provide, students should write a multi-paragraph essay. Some will not be ready for this, others will. At the very least, it will confirm their mastery of (to continue your example) capitalization, and at best it will give the teacher insight into other literacy skills that need extra attention. I would note parenthetically that you must avoid any assessment program that relies exclusively on multiple choice testing. I've done extensive research on this. The best way to improve performance on state test scores, including state multiple-choice test scores, is more student nonfiction writing, provided that this writing is scored collaboratively by teachers using a rubric and students use the feedback to revise and improve their writing.

Show Me the Proof

27 **How do you know that your company's standards-based performance assessments really work?**

First, it is true that we have had many clients over the years who have demonstrated significant progress after increasing the quality and quantity of their standards-based performance assessments. They even are kind enough to say that our professional development on Power Standards, assessments, leadership, and other support was helpful to them in achieving those results. We document many of these cases in every issue of our newsletter, *Focus on Achievement*, and we'd be happy to offer a free subscription to you if you would like. We find this documentation useful, but it is more a reflection of the hard work of our clients than any claim on our part to influence test scores.

Second, we have never—absolutely never—claimed that we were the singular cause of improved test scores or other measurements of student achievement. Teachers, students, parents, and leaders cause improvements in achievement, and you should beware of the outside consultant who claims credit for your work. What we can say definitively is that we have a solid track record of improving the knowledge and skills of educators and school leaders in the areas of standards, assessment, and accountability. When they combine those skills and knowledge with consistent implementation, it is frequently the case that student achievement improves. Our work in Riverview Gardens, Norfolk, Orange County, Waukesha, and Wayne Township are just a few of the hundreds of school systems throughout the United States and other countries where we have a record of improving the knowledge and skills of educators and leaders and where, at the same time, student achievement has improved. But let us be clear: Those hardworking teachers and leaders and students and parents caused the improvement, not us. It is also true that many other things influence test scores, and anyone who claims that there is a single cause of test score changes has not spent much time around a school or classroom.

Third, there is a large body of research that suggests an association between the greater use of performance assesment and improved academic achievement. One of the best summaries of that research is the first 100 pages of Linda Darling-Hammond's excellent book, *The Right to Learn*. You can also find articles on our web site, www.MakingStandardsWork. com, that summarize some of the Center's research that associates writing performance assessment with higher academic achievement in math, science, and social studies. We never rely on a single study or source, including our own work, to make a conclusion, but rather rely on the preponderance of the evidence gathered over many years that says standards-based performance assessment is a good idea.

Fourth, even if we had not a shred of statistical evidence to support the use of standards-based assessments, we would still advocate their use because we believe it is morally the right thing to do. We believe that students and teachers are entitled to fairness, and fairness requires that the rules of the academic game are clear, not mysterious. Standards, when properly implemented, let every student, parent, and teacher know what success means and how to achieve it. By creating a continuum of performance to include exemplary levels, we also challenge students who are already meeting standards while at the same time giving clear and fair guidelines to students who are not yet meeting standards. We believe that this is the fairest way to conduct a classroom, school, and district, and thus on ethical grounds we favor transparent and clear assessments at the classroom level and throughout the system.

So, can we "prove" that our brand-name staff development makes test scores go up? No. We don't have to, and even if we tried, such an assertion is preposterous. As an increasingly ancient former statistics professor reminds us, "life is multivariate," and there is never a single cause for a complex effect in human affairs.

Finally, even if you don't believe a single word I've said, don't let it make you go back to the bell curve. If I don't produce a study that satisfactorily supports writing and the connection between literacy and other subjects, don't conclude that literacy is a bad idea and that your students do not need to write better. In other words, are you completely satisfied the way things are now? If so, we can't help people who are completely satisfied and have no desire to change the results they are achieving. But if you are dissatisfied with results, then you must also be willing to change methods, including assessment and instruction. You don't need an outside consultant to suggest that you cannot continue to do the same things and expect different results.

28 **I am a teacher and I need research backing up your International Performance Assessment System (IPAS). Do you have any resources you may e-mail me or direct me to on the internet?**

There is a significant body of research supporting the use of performance assessments to improve student achievement. The best assembly of this is by Linda Darling-Hammond of Stanford in the book, *The Right to Learn* (Jossey-Bass, 1997). In the first 100 pages, she provides a mountain of evidence linking performance assessment with better student achievement. You can also find similar research in many articles and books I have written, many of which are available as free downloads on our web site at www.MakingStandardsWork. com. I would never claim that IPAS or any other single assessment is a cause for improved student achievement. What is certainly true is that performance assessment and, more particularly, performance assessment requiring student writing is linked to improved student achievement in every academic area.

Finally, I think we need to ask what the alternative is to performance assessment: multiple-choice tests, true/false exams, and casual observations. Only when there is a clear standard of performance and a continuum of performance levels,such as IPAS and other good performance assessments provide, can students, parents, and teachers have a clear idea of what successful academic performance really means.

Reading and Student Achievement

29 In your book, *Accountability in Action,* you state that increased time on reading in the curriculum can lead to higher test scores in science, even when time spent on science is decreased. I know that some of the high-stakes tests have science components that enable the better readers to succeed because the science information is supplied in a text form. The students can simply glean the information out of the test material to find the correct answer. Our Stanford-9 exams were largely of this sort. This would, of course, enable the better readers to score higher on the exam.

But what of the tests that rely on questions that refer to material that was learned in the classroom and not supplied in the test material? To which of these two kinds of tests does your data refer? Are scores higher even for those tests in which students must know the material prior to taking the test? If so, how can this be?

In this case, students were also required to take tests in science and social studies content. The same was also true of schools in Virginia that replicated these results. Even when schools reduced their science curriculum to one day each week, the science scores increased. This is strikingly similar to results in a California study where the Stanford-9 science test was used. The students who overemphasized literacy, particularly nonfiction writing (including writing ABOUT SCIENCE) with editing and rewriting, had higher Stanford-9 science scores than students who simply "covered the curriculum."

The other component of improved science scores is a focus on the right thing. Students need time every week to ask questions, develop hypotheses, make systematic observations, record those observations on tables, charts, or graphs, draw inferences from those graphs, and then write a report about it. This is better achieved in a single 90-minute science block each week than a frantic attempt to cover rocks, clouds, and volcanoes in forty-five minutes every day. I'm not discounting science at all. Rather, I am emphasizing the most important parts of science: creating and testing hypotheses, gathering data, and drawing appropriate conclusions from those data points. But none of that matters if kids can't read the question. No doubt about it: Literacy is more important.

30 **Have you done any research, or do you know of any that has been done, that studies the effect of reading nonfiction (versus reading narrative fiction) on students' vocabulary development? Also, I'm interested in resources on the positive effects that writing nonfiction has on student achievement.**

I'm not aware of distinctions between fiction and nonfiction on vocabulary development. However, I did just complete an accountability study (to be published later this year by ASCD) in which secondary social studies and science classes that used "word walls" (quite similar to those used in early primary grades) had significant gains in state science and social studies tests. I also just finished Bob Marzano's splendid new book, *What Works in Schools* (ASCD, 2003) and he specifically addresses the value of direct instruction vocabulary development as a superior alternative to attempting to learn vocabulary solely through exposure to words through reading.

There are quite a number of sources that link writing to improved student achievement. The article "Standards are not enough" in the December 2000 issue of the NASSP *Bulletin* is a good place to start. In addition, see the new 2002 Jossey-Bass books *The Leader's Guide to Standards* and *The Daily Disciplines of Leadership*. See also Vicki Spandel's writing as well as that by Lucy Calkins (*The Art of Teaching Writing* is a good place to start). Finally, Linda Darling-Hammond's excellent book *The Right to Learn* provides abundant evidence of the link between nonfiction writing through authentic performance assessment and improved student achievement.

31 Last year, our school began using a new reading program in grades K-3 in an effort to bring all students up to their appropriate grade level in reading and improve our reading scores on the state test. The new program is a Pearson Learning program based on levelled readers, running records, and Direct Reading Assessment (DRA). We use the program along with Accelerated Reader, the STAR (a computerized CLOZE-based placement test), and the Tests for Higher Standards. We believed that all of these components would go together to present a cohesive picture of student achievement. So far, we are getting erratic results on the various assessments, and they do not seem consistent with how the students do on the state test. What can we do to make sure that all of the components are giving us a valid picture of what we need to work on before the students take the state test?

First, congratulations on your exceptional focus on reading. You are doing the right thing. I understand your frustration about the different results from different assessments, but there is a rational explanation for this that I will address in a moment. The most important thing, however, is that you are focused on literacy, and that is essential for success on state tests and every other challenge that your students will face.

Second, different assessments focus on different things, even if they all bear the label "reading test." Some that you mentioned focus on word attack skills and oral reading, while others focus on reading comprehension, principally factual recall. Other tests, such as most state tests, emphasize summarization, inferences, synthesis, and prediction. Therefore, teachers must think about what "good reading" really means. They must recognize that it is a combination of many different skills, and it is entirely possible for a student to make great progress on decoding and word attack, and still lag behind in comprehension; that explains the difference between the DRA and state test results, for example. It is not that the DRA is bad, but it is not sufficient. You need ALL of these assessments and you need to attain proficiency in ALL of them.

Third, ensure that all teachers are administering the assessments in a similar way. I have noticed that some teachers tend to give students far more assistance than others during the assessments. When they do this, the students receive a higher score in the short run, but then fail when they have to work independently, as they do on state tests.

Fourth, do not forget the importance of writing. If you want to focus on reading comprehension skills, have students write about what they have been reading.

32 **Could you please provide me with information regarding silent reading's benefits over oral reading in the classroom? I am making a claim that oral reading is detrimental to the self esteem of children who struggle because they are embarrassed to read in front of a class. I also claim that oral reading tends not to cater to students who have short attention spans. Are these claims valid?**

First, the most definitive research on the reading issue has to do with independent reading. Either oral or silent reading can be effective, provided that it is consistent, of at least twenty minutes' duration, and conducted independently. Of course, we have no way of knowing if it is effective if students do not talk about or write about their reading. Therefore, I recommend that immediately after that twenty minutes, students should briefly (five minutes is enough) write about the main idea of that day's reading and then explain (also in writing) how it is similar to or different from the previous day's reading.

With regard to the issue of silent or oral reading, perhaps we can find a middle ground. My concern with the extreme of "don't read aloud if it's uncomfortable" is that someone will, ultimately, expect students to read aloud and speak with confidence, clarity, and precision. We do students no favors by avoiding this task. Rather, we should "set them up for success," giving reluctant readers passages to read with which they are comfortable and confident. Sometimes passages of poetry or familiar song lyrics will fill this requirement. Other times, passages of the students' own writing will be appropriate. In any case, students must be able to both read silently and read aloud, and in both cases, they must demonstrate that they have comprehended the written material. The best way for that demonstration to occur is a written summary of the main ideas and supporting details of what they have read, or an appropriate graphic organizer of the ideas contained in the reading passage.

Finally, let me address the attention span issue. Before we conclude that a student has a short attention span, I would want to watch how long the student remains engaged in other tasks. If, for example, they can play basketball for fifteen minutes, play Nintendo for forty-five minutes, but can only read for five minutes, then we should ask, "What is it about basketball and Nintendo that keeps this student engaged?" It might be the clarity of the requirements for success and the frequency of the feedback. It certainly is not the inability to attend to a task.

Reading Programs

33 **We are researching reading programs successfully implemented by high schools to improve student reading comprehension as we attempt to design a program that will work for us. Any ideas on a specific program and/or school I should contact?**

With regard to high school reading comprehension, I would be less inclined to use a scripted program than to use techniques that can be applied in many different high school subjects. Examples of activities that can be integrated into your current curriculum without the cost of purchasing a separate program include the following:

1. Summaries. In social studies and science classes, require students to write brief summaries of one or two page textbook passages. These summaries need not be formal essays. It is sufficient to have them write the "main idea" and

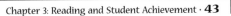

then "three or more supporting details." This is also an excellent way to get better value out of time devoted to SSR—Sustained Silent Reading—at the high school level.

2. Similarities and differences. This is particularly helpful when students are reading accounts of historical events or scientific observations.

3. Graphic organizers. To demonstrate student understanding of complex literary structures, including novels, plays, and poems, students can use graphic organizers (See Marzano & Pickering's *Classroom Instruction That Works*) to illustrate the patterns of events, settings, and characters.

4. Inferences. When students review a graph in a math, science, physical education, or social studies class, they should write a three to four sentence explanation that elaborates on the meaning of the graph and the relationship among the variables.

5. Compare and contrast. In art classes, students can compare and contrast different artistic styles or the characteristics of different artistic media.

6. Strategies and rules. In PE and technology classes, students can describe which strategies are most effective for various athletic and electronic games.

This is a start. The key is that when students do more writing, with editing and rewriting, their performance improves in every academic subject. A recent *Education Week* report by Kathleen Manzo indicated that 63 percent of high school students never complete a research paper requiring footnotes and bibliographies. This failure to challenge students to think, research, and write is directly associated with the failures of students in college and technical school.

For very recent information on the value of writing for ALL students, see Dr. Mel Levine's new book, *The Myth of Laziness*. I have also addressed this in my books, *The Daily Disciplines of Leadership* and *The Leader's Guide to Standards*.

34 **I am interested in knowing what experience you may have with the Accelerated Reading Program. Accelerated Reader is utilized in grades 3-5 currently. Do you have any data related to its impact on achievement?**

As is true of most programs, the advocates have mounds of data and testimonials which assert that the program is effective, while the critics can always find instances in which the program was installed and had no impact at all on student achievement. Thus we come to one of the primary conclusions you can almost always make about program evaluation: It's not the brand name, but the professional practices that have the real impact on student achievement. This is the same whether you had asked about Success for All, Direct Instruction, Accelerated Reader, or any number of programs. When they are associated with improved student achievement, you will find a faculty and principal that enthusiastically embraced the program, used it frequently, carefully tracked progress, shared success stories and disappointments, and made numerous midcourse corrections in order to ensure that the program was successful. Where the very same program was unsuccessful, the contents of the magic box were the same, but the professional practices and leadership behaviors were vastly different.

My own observations of Accelerated Reader have been most positive when the teacher places a strong emphasis on reading comprehension, often by having students write about each book before taking the computerized test. Student writing includes summarization (essentials of comprehension), analysis (comparing one book or character to other books and characters), and inferences (drawing conclusions that are not readily apparent from the facts of the text). In these schools, principals closely monitored not only the accumulated AR points, but also the specific practices that were associated with student success. They identified and documented success stories as part of an ongoing pattern of faculty collaboration. Finally, the leaders systematically related the results in AR to the results achieved by the students on other reading assessments.

You might say, "Gee, if the faculty and principal did all of those things with just plain old library books and without an outside program, student achievement might have increased." That's the entire point. There is nothing wrong with AR, but in the end, it's what the teachers and principals do that matters most.

35 **Do you think Sustained Silent Reading is essential for student success, or is it just an ineffective, unstructured time for students to daydream? I have colleagues that claim that, especially for our more underprivileged kids, it is a waste of time.**

Clearly, the more appropriate conclusion is that any program—SSR or anything else—is only as good as the teacher who is implementing it. Yes, it should be long-term, rigorously controlled, related to content, and grade-level appropriate. In my judgment, it should be followed up with five minutes of writing ABOUT what they have read, so that teachers have instantaneous feedback on whether the reading material was appropriate and whether students can comprehend what they are "reading."

So, quoting a "pro-SSR" study is not an argument in favor of ANY SSR, but of well-constructed and professionally implemented SSR. Quoting an "anti-SSR" study is not an argument against SSR, but an argument against BAD TEACHING.

There can no doubt be arguments made against my studies, even though I have tons of confirmation and large samples, somebody (particularly somebody who is constitutionally unable to acknowledge that poor and minority kids can do well) will always find something wrong with students that fail to support their prejudices. So I ask them, what is the risk that I am WRONG, and you go ahead and give kids extra literacy training that they didn't need? The risk, I guess, is "overly literate" students who have "too much literacy" and "extra unnecessary preparation" for the next level of schooling. I don't hear those complaints very frequently. What is the risk if I am RIGHT, and we fail to give kids the extra literacy that they need? The research here is unambiguous. When students are non-proficient 8th grade readers, there is an 85 percent probability that they remain non-proficient throughout high school.

I'm used to people taking pot shots at research. There is no substitute for great teachers and hard work and MORE TIME on reading and writing. Where people do those things, we see higher achievement and a closing equity gap. Where people are paralyzed or where they fail to implement additional literacy instruction because the research supporting it might be imperfect, they continue to engage in the same wasteland of ineffective techniques they have been using in the past.

In sum, I'm not supporting mindless SSR that is unstructured and without accountability. But I'm a big fan of MORE reading and MORE writing, provided the reading is appropriate to the student and the writing includes editing, rewriting, and collaborative scoring. Knowing what we do about student motivation, I'd probably figure out a way to incorporate some independent selection into that process as well.

36 **I am an English teacher at the high school level who has recently been having problems with a new principal. Our new principal states that he questions my assigning fifteen to twenty minutes (out of ninety minutes) of class time to silent reading and doubts it promotes learning. I am in search of information to support silent reading and the positive effects that it creates. If you know of any journal articles or research papers to help me in this "proof" of benefits, please let me know.**

The direct answer to your question is a 1988 article in the *Reading Research Quarterly* (see the full citation in the Reference section of this book) that noted that students who read independently for twenty minutes each day had dramatically higher reading scores than students who did not. While this research has been used to support SSR, I think it's a stretch. Students who choose to read independently ON THEIR OWN are quite different from those in the classroom where independent reading is contrived. Of course, we have to start the habit in some way.

I think I can offer a solution that will satisfy you and the principal. Many schools use it and it's called "Power SSR." Students read independently for fifteen minutes, and then stop and answer two questions in writing: 1) What did you read about today? and 2) How was today's reading similar to or different from yesterday's reading?

This provides accountability for you and the principal. If students don't actually read, you catch it. It requires little or no time; you can just scan the papers as students are writing them. It's strictly S/U evaluation: Either they answer the questions or they don't. You don't even have to enter these in the grade book. But the consequence for failing to answer the questions is that you select their reading and supervise their reading. Adolescents crave independence and freedom more than they do grades. If they do choose their own stuff, they'll have to take the reading seriously and be able to summarize what they have read. This is differentiated instruction at its best: Some students love SSR, others can't handle it or require closer supervision. This allows you to individualize your approach to meet student learning needs.

It also allows you to make appropriate referrals if you think that a student might have a learning disability that affects reading, and you catch it much earlier than you would if you were relying on traditional testing.

37 **Recently at a conference I was told there has been new research done on SSR being used in conjunction with writing. I was told that the research shows no gain made in schools using SSR unless there was the component of writing added to the SSR time. Where can I find this research?**

I am not at all familiar with the research you heard, but I can offer two observations. First, there is a substantial body of research on the value of independent reading for a minimum of twenty minutes per day. This is hardly new—it's why so many people do SSR. The problem, of course, is that what a lot of people call "SSR" is not independent reading, but twenty minutes of unstructured, disorganized, and wasted time. The fact remains; independent reading is a good idea.

Second, there is also a substantial body of research that supports the relationship of writing—particularly nonfiction writing, including summarization of nonfiction text—and improved student achievement in reading, math, social studies, and science. You can find that research summarized in articles I have written (downloadable at www.MakingStandardsWork.com) as well as in Linda Darling-Hammond's book, *The Right to Learn*.

A couple of footnotes for your consideration: Educational research is almost never one-sided. The best approach is to look at the preponderance of the evidence and consider many different studies, not a single one. Finally, let common sense be your guide. We really don't need statistical studies to say that reading is important for kids, nor do we need statistical studies to say that every implementation of a program (writing, reading, or anything else) is only as good as the teachers implementing them. The label we attach to the program is not as important as the professional practices of teachers. Thus some SSR will be fabulous and directly support student achievement, while other SSR will be awful and a waste of time. It is the teachers that make the difference. I like linking writing to SSR because it makes sense, combines the research on the value of reading and the value of writing, and gives kids a necessary summarization skill that is frequently tested and used throughout their lives.

38 **I find it difficult to have SSR with my 3rd graders. Some just flip through a book and say, 'I'm done.' Others need to use the bathroom, get a tissue, etc. to try and use up the thirty minutes. Only a few actually read. I am frustrated!**

Although in theory Sustained Silent Reading (SSR) is a great idea, the practical implementation can be a challenge. First, let's remember why we do SSR in the first place. About sixteen years ago, a large-scale study found that students who read independently at least twenty minutes each day scored almost eighty percentile points higher in national reading tests than students who did not. Of course, students who choose to read independently probably have a lot of other skills in literacy and time management than students who do not, and there may be many other differences. Moreover, genuine independent reading is not the same as contrived independent reading. Nevertheless, it is the attempt to create independent readers that is behind SSR.

Now, how to make it work? Here are some ideas.

Kids are motivated by freedom and choice. But freedom and choice come at a price. At the end of each SSR period, have students answer two questions in writing for five minutes. What did you read about today? How is today's reading similar to or different from yesterday's reading? You don't even have to collect the papers, but can simply walk around the classroom. Students who answer those two questions will get to continue to choose their own reading material for SSR tomorrow. Students who do not will have reading directed by the teacher. In other cases, students who cannot focus on the material for twenty to thirty minutes will be assigned to a dyad or appropriate small group with teacher leadership. When they complain that they want to be able to read alone and choose their own material, then all they need to do is answer the two questions well for three consecutive days, and they gain the freedom to read again.

39 **How should SSR as a high school-wide initiative be implemented? Does research support reading improvement as a result of SSR? What diagnostic test could be administered before and during the initiative to monitor improvement? Would it be effective for every student in the school to read at the same designated time twenty minutes, twice weekly? How many minutes does research show as being productive? Could the SSR rubric provided in _Making Standards Work_ be calculated as a grade?**

 I agree strongly with your idea for Sustained Silent

Reading in high school IF you meet the following criteria:

1. There is immediate assessment by the supervising teacher to ensure that students are actually reading, and that they understand what they read. This can be as simple as having students maintain a reading journal in which they answer two questions after fifteen minutes of reading—first, "What did you read about today?" and second "How was today's reading similar to or different from what you read yesterday?" If students cannot answer those questions, then the supervising teacher needs to take a much more active role in determining how to assist that student to select appropriate reading material, or move that student to a supervised group for reading intervention. This is definitely NOT a "one size fits all" strategy, and if students are not able to read alone successfully, you can't waste twenty minutes of valuable instructional time.

2. I also agree with doing some assessment of student reading skills. Norfolk has a number of quick and easy reading comprehension assessments available to schools in the Division. Some are administered on the computer, and others by teachers. As a general principle, it's more important to get feedback very frequently and quickly, particularly for students who are struggling with reading. To save teachers time and hassle, you might want to have a rule that once a student is reading on, say, grade level 10 or higher, then they are exempt from additional reading assessments. But for high school students who are testing at reading level 9 or lower, they should be receiving intensive assistance and counselors should ensure that their schedule includes mandatory reading and literacy support classes. It just doesn't make sense to have a student who is reading on a 7th grade level sitting in high school classes using books he can't read, and then wait for a 9th or 10th grade failure before the system intervenes decisively.

3. For monitoring, how about a simple chart that shows "Percentage of students reading at or above grade level" that

you update every quarter? This could be displayed along with other charts, such as "Percentage of students passing" and "Percentage of students making adequate progress toward the next grade level" or "percentage of students attending 90 percent or more of classes."

This does not have to be an elaborate or time-consuming system—we just want to be sure that students are reading, reading on grade level, and reading with comprehension.

Finally, I think that the SSR does NOT need to involve completely free choice. Students can earn free choice by having B or better work in their classes. If they are not earning a B or better, perhaps you should consider requiring that the SSR is focused on a subject where they need particular assistance. It's just a brainstorm for you and the faculty to consider.

40 **I am looking for practices used with SSR, how the time for SSR might fit into a block schedule, and actual statistics from a school that has actually implemented an SSR program and experienced an increase in reading levels, to support the approval of an SSR program at the high school level. Any help would be appreciated.**

The best SSR practices I have seen recently involve a combination of reading and writing, as well as a combination of student-directed and teacher-directed reading.

First, reading alone without a writing component fails to help students improve synthesis skills, one of the keys to effective reading comprehension. Thus if you have a twenty-minute SSR, ideally you should have fifteen minutes of reading, followed by five minutes in which students answer two questions:

1. What did you read about today?

2. How was today's reading similar to or different from yesterday's reading?

You need not grade these papers, but can simply look around the classroom and see who is able to coherently respond to them. Students who can't write about what they are reading are probably not reading material that is appropriate or interesting. It's a clear sign that the teacher needs to intervene and help select reading material and provide more direct instructional assistance for that student.

The original SSR studies (that provided the statistics you request) showed that students who read independently for twenty minutes each day scored as many as eighty percentile points higher on standardized reading tests as students who did not. But this ASSUMES that the students, of their own volition, chose to read for twenty minutes each day. That assumption says a lot not only about what is happening for those twenty minutes, but about the rest of that child's home life for many years prior to that study. It is no wonder that they had higher reading scores. It doesn't follow, however, that then contriving to have students hold a magazine or book for twenty unstructured minutes will yield the same results as that study.

Students who are not used to selecting appropriate reading material, thinking about what they have read, and relating that reading to other contexts and previous reading, will need some assistance. This is an opportunity for you to provide differentiation in the most appropriate sense. Everyone is working on reading, but the structure, content, and supervision will vary widely depending on the needs of individual students.

Show Me the Proof

 41 **I am aware of many resources on writing, but specifically wanted resources on reading comprehension and test scores. I understand that you have stressed expository text: reading shorter works such as articles in depth instead of just a lot of longer, fictional novels. Where in your works or articles could I find this information?**

Here are several resources to consider:

- Calkins, Lucy, *The Art of Teaching Reading* (Longman, 2000)

- Darling-Hammond, Linda, *The Right to Learn* (Jossey-Bass, 1997)

- Reeves, D., "Standards are not enough." (NASSP *Bulletin*, December 2000)

- Reeves, D., *The Leader's Guide to Standards* (Jossey-Bass, 2003)

- Reeves, D., *The Daily Disciplines of Leadership* (Jossey-Bass, 2003)

- Reeves, D., *Reason to Write* (Simon & Schuster, 2002)

- Reeves D., *Accountability in Action* (Advanced Learning Press, 2000)

Even without this research, most teachers I know are quite clear that the fundamental need of their students is to comprehend what is in the textbook, and the best way to promote nonfiction comprehension is for students to write summaries, including main idea and supporting details, of what they read. Without question, the most common feedback I receive from teachers in college and technical school is that students must improve writing skills.

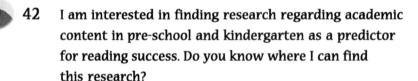 **42 I am interested in finding research regarding academic content in pre-school and kindergarten as a predictor for reading success. Do you know where I can find this research?**

There are several studies on the value of early academic content, but the specific study that I cited was written by Kurdek and Sinclair and published in the *Journal of Educational Psychology*, September 2001. It's entitled "Predicting reading and mathematic achievement in 5th grade children from kindergarten readiness scores."

For a technical treatment of various policy implications of kindergarten and early childhood reading, see Timothy Hacsi's splendid book, *Children as Pawns*. He provides a thorough review of the research literature on this subject. For a teacher-friendly book that is one of the best I have ever read on the subject, see Lucy Calkins' *Lessons from a Child* and *The Art of Teaching Writing*. You might consider a book by a guy named Reeves entitled *Reason to Write* and the *Reason to Write Student Handbook*. All of these titles should be available at your local book stores or on Amazon.com.

Writing and Student Achievement

The Best Types of Writing for Student Achievement

43   **I am trying to convince my principal that our students should be required to do some nonfiction writing every day. He says he will only agree to it if I can prove that it will raise test scores, and most of our tests are multiple choice. Do you have any evidence you can supply me with?**

The original article on this was from the NASSP *Bulletin*, December 2000, entitled "Standards Are Not Enough." I have amplified on this theme in the new books, *The Leader's Guide to Standards* and *The Daily Disciplines of Leadership* recently published by Jossey-Bass. Linda Darling-Hammond's wonderful book, *The Right to Learn*, also uses many citations to support this theme. You can also show your principal Robert Marzano's work. In *Classroom Instruction that Works*, almost all of the dependent variables were multiple choice test scores, yet none of the nine strategies were classical multiple choice test prep. Of those most related to our writing work, the note-taking, similarities and differences, and graphic organizers are all directly related to the writing processes that we advocate.

Of course, at the end of the day, it isn't just footnotes that resolve this issue, but common sense. What do students really need to improve test scores? Not mindless test prep, but thinking, reasoning, and analysis. Writing about things such as "why the wrong answer is wrong" gives students the analytical ability that they need to become better communicators and to excel at multiple choice questions. As is the case with all research, it isn't perfect, so at the end of the day, one must ask, "What is the risk if the research is wrong?" We might have students who do "too much" writing and would thus presumably become "too literate." But if the research is right and we fail to give students additional literacy and nonfiction writing, editing, and rewriting, then there is a lifetime of adverse consequences for them.

I also encourage you and your principal to conduct your own case studies and action research to test these hypotheses. See if the students who do a great deal more literacy in science, for example, wind up with lower science scores. See if students who write summaries of each sub-chapter in a social studies book are irreparably damaged. The real issue is whether these strategies are more dangerous for student learning than the strategies that you are using now. Your principal should not need a set of perfect research to suggest that change is needed.

44 **The Language Arts teachers in my district are confused as to what is meant by 'nonfiction writing.' For the most part, the elementary and middle school staff thinks of this as anything related to content in reading, math, science, and social studies. This would also include biography and autobiography. The high school staff felt that if the students were reading a fiction piece and then doing research (they called this literary analysis) and read other pieces of information about it and wrote a paper, this was nonfiction writing. My question is: Isn't nonfiction writing related to informational reading and not a piece of fiction? If their literary analysis is written in this format, is that nonfiction writing?**

By "nonfiction" I mean the entire range of writing that includes description (with rich and specific detail), persuasion (with evidence and argumentation), analysis (compare and contrast), and technical (process description, ideal for technology, math, and physical education). Of course, biography, literary analysis, and a host of other things are appropriate as well. My main concern in this area stems from two things. First, I did a content analysis a couple of years ago of 3rd grade writing and found a 90:1 ratio of fiction to nonfiction. Students then went to future classes where they were expected to be able to compare, contrast, describe, and persuade, and were totally unprepared for it. I am certainly not diminishing the need for fiction and poetry, but only asking for a more reasonable balance than is typically the case now.

When it comes to writing in the content areas, there a couple of things you may wish to consider to gain greater cooperation from all faculty members. First, consider a simplified school-wide writing rubric, particularly for middle and high school. This would be less complex than the language arts rubric (I'm not too concerned about the use of passive voice in a geometry proof). It would, however, make clear that in ANY subject, students at least must have a coherent organization and adhere to reasonable conventions of Standard English. Second, consider using "two-column" grading in the content areas, so that a science teacher can, for example, distinguish between the quality of the scientific analysis and the written expression of that analysis. "Your interpretation of the experimental results was excellent, but your lab report is so difficult to read that you need to rewrite it with better attention to organization and spelling." By the time a 10th grade history teacher is requiring written responses to document-based questions, students (who began approaching such problems in elementary school) should be able to say, "been there, done that" and thus not be as traumatized as most high school students are when confronted with writing requirements in the content areas.

Just one more note of perspective. At the Cleveland airport, I spent half an hour on the phone with the curriculum director of a university town with supposedly high-performing students, and they adamantly refused to consider having any of our people talk about writing in the content areas. "Informal" writing was fine, he said, but writing with feedback, editing, and rewriting so that lab reports were coherent and historical analyses were understandable? Out of the question. If I seem a bit strident at times, it is because conversations like that one push me over the edge.

45 Do you have any caveats about middle school field trips in light of the standards movement?

The threshold question is, "Is it worth writing about?" I know of very high performing schools that have a minimum of two field trips every year (and I mean trips to the ocean, to the mountains, to something extraordinary). These are not merely vacations, but exceptional opportunities to weave together the students' knowledge of science, social studies, reading, and writing.

So, a trip to the pizza parlor for fun? No. A trip to the museum, symphony, or the ocean to discover a world that they did not know existed, and about which they will write for extended periods of time? Absolutely.

 46 **Please answer one question for me. If I have limited language arts time is it justified for me to use twenty minutes each day for journal writing that isn't assessed?**

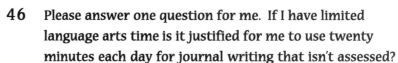 Journal writing can be helpful IF it meets these criteria:

1. Students use it as part of the writing process. This means that they get feedback, extend their ideas, and proceed from brainstorming, to organizers, to outline, to draft, and ultimately to final copy.

2. Students use the journal as evidence of improved writing, including word choice, organization, and conventions. Contrary to popular myth, the rules of good written expression apply even for journals. This doesn't mean all entries must be perfect, but it does mean that this is PART of the process and entries that are rough must be eventually rewritten.

 47 **My principal and I are attempting to 'nudge' writing in our school in a positive direction, and we wanted your input.**
    First, a committee sent out a survey to the entire staff. How much writing is everyone doing, what form does the writing take, how is the writing assessed, and so on? It came as no surprise to me that our results were very positive. We have a good staff and a good school. Writing is happening throughout the building. Now, how do we make it better, and where do we go from here?

The committee has planned a very basic follow-up activity for our upcoming in-service day. Teachers will sit in on their colleagues' classrooms (sans students!) to hear about successful writing strategies, techniques, and procedures that are utilized. The goal is to establish a starting point for discussion, for sharing, and for fostering an atmosphere of academic dialogue among the staff. Your thoughts?

Your ideas are terrific. I particularly appreciate the idea of devoting a professional development day to teachers sharing their own success stories with one another. This case study approach is professional, based in action research, and much more credible than a dozen outside abstract studies that may not be relevant to your students. Let me offer some ideas to enhance the day:

First, get a wide variety of teachers to participate. Writing cannot be the exclusive domain of the Language Arts faculty. Just this week I heard from a music teacher who has students writing every week about compositions, the meaning of lyrics, the intent of the composers, and the similarities and differences among various pieces of music they have studied. Teachers in art, PE, technology, world languages, and career/tech prep should all have the opportunity to share their success stories, as well as people in math, science, and social studies.

Second, ask for "hyper-specificity." The success stories should include actual examples of student work (without names, of course), the scoring rubric that was used, the specific writing prompts or tasks that were required, and so on. Success studies are most helpful when a teacher who was not there and does not have great familiarity with the subject can say, "You have given me enough information so that I can do this in my class."

Third, give yourself some time to look for trends. After analyzing and synthesizing all the success stories, what do you notice? Some things that I have seen in these cases include:

- When the rubric is more specific, teachers are more likely to agree on what "proficient" means.

- When teachers collaborated, they had less work in grading and more focused tasks by the students.

- In middle school in particular, the greatest success occurred when students had the CONSISTENT set of writing requirements in every subject.

- Administrators gave teachers TIME to do these tasks and TIME to collaborate, including time in faculty meetings, time in staff development, and time in grade level or department meetings. These were never used for announcements, but for examination of real student work.

- Consistency—the best success stories were not the result of one-shot attempts at writing, but rather the result of focused and consistent emphasis over the course of many months or years.

48 **I am having discussions with my staff about the increase in non-fiction writing in an elementary setting. We are wondering more specifically, what that would look like? I have downloaded the sample assessments from the websites, but was wondering if there are more sample non-fiction writing activities that we could look at from the 90/90/90 schools.**

You can find specific samples of student work in the paperbacks, *Reason to Write* and the *Reason to Write Student Handbook*. They are available for $14 and $12 respectively in all major bookstores.

In general, students focused on descriptive, analytical, and persuasive writing. They used the same scoring rubric, usually created by the students and teacher based on the state writing standards.

The key, of course, is the process—graphic organizer, outline, draft, edit, revise—sometimes with multiple edits and revisions.

One school asked each teacher to write down during a faculty meeting three favorite nonfiction writing prompts on any subject. The principal just collected those and published them—the topics were applicable for more than a single grade level, and teachers immediately had more than fifty writing prompts.

To get started, teachers can simply have students start with descriptive writing:

1. Describe the rules of a game (in physical education class, perhaps?)

2. Describe a work of art

3. Describe a musical piece

Then move to analytical writing, comparing one story (or character or setting or country or state) to another, noting similarities and differences.

Then move to persuasive writing, noting the difference between supporting an argument with feelings and supporting an argument with facts and evidence.

Of course, there is still a place for fiction and personal narratives, but most elementary classrooms are way out of balance, with one I studied having a 90:1 ratio of fiction to nonfiction writing. I'm just asking for balance: more nonfiction writing than we typically have now.

 49 **We are looking for research that shows the impact writing has on math achievement. I understand that you have some research supporting the importance of writing and achievement. Do you have articles or research you would be willing to share regarding this topic?**

 There is a lot of literature on this. See, for example:

- Calkins, Lucy, *The Art of Teaching Writing* (Heinemann, 1996)

- Darling-Hammond, Linda, *The Right to Learn* (Jossey-Bass, 1997)

- Reeves, D., "Standards are not enough." (NASSP *Bulletin*, December 2000)

- Reeves, D., *The Daily Disciplines of Leadership* (Jossey-Bass, 2003)

- Reeves, D., *Reason to Write* (Simon & Schuster, 2002)

Remember that we are not talking about aimless writing here, particularly in math class. It is writing directly connected to the curriculum. For example, I have students:

1. Write about why a WRONG answer is wrong on a math multiple choice test. I want them to get into the mind of the test writer and understand the distracter responses and explain why they might look attractive, why they are wrong, and how to get the right answer.

2. Write a test question that is directly linked to a standard.

3. Write a performance task that is directly linked to a standard.

4. Write a scoring guide that is linked to the task in (3) above. Explain precisely what a "proficient" response would be.

5. Explain in words what inferences and conclusions I should draw from a graph or chart. If I changed the formula for the data display, how would that change the inferences I can draw? There are many variations on this theme: change from linear to nonlinear, etc.

Support for Student Writing

50 **The administration has asked us to make sure our students do more writing. Many of the teachers in my school are resistant and feel the 'requirements' from the administration are not aligned with their content, and therefore are reluctant to learn and grow. Can you help?**

There are several ways to work with subject-matter specialists in secondary schools to gain improved cooperation in student writing.

First, let's make clear that we are not trying to make every teacher into an English teacher. The evidence on the relationship between improved writing and higher student achievement in math, science, reading, and social studies makes clear that we are not doing writing to avoid math or the other content areas, but rather we are doing writing to improve student achievement in all content areas.

Second, we can compromise on what "writing" means in the content areas. Frankly, I'll settle for "two-trait" writing—just organization and conventions. Every teacher, regardless of academic background, can help students express their thoughts with a clear beginning, middle, and end, and they can do so with correct spelling, grammar, and punctuation. Don't ask me to worry about passive voice, expressive voice, or the perfect metaphor. Just focus on organization and conventions. That's a reasonable compromise.

Third, embrace team assessments and team scoring. If a content teacher doesn't want to do writing, then make it acceptable for them to create a joint assessment with another teacher in which one teacher scores content and another scores written expression.

Fourth, stop calling it "writing" and start calling it "thinking, reasoning, analysis, and communication." Content teachers are not writing teachers, perhaps, but they certainly are teachers of thinking, analysis, reasoning, and communication. High-performing schools require student writing in every—and I mean every (PE, home economics, technology, welding, music, art, science, etc.)—area at least once per semester, and I know of some schools that require it every month.

51 **Do you have a few tips for high school parents who want to support the school's writing focus at home? I am noting the *Reason to Write* as a possible resource.**

Parents of teens may think that their days of influence are almost over. As the parent of a couple of teenagers, I know that I feel that way, too, on some days. Nevertheless, parents remain the most important influence in the lives of their children. By their daily lives and models, not just their words, parents are more important than peers, teachers, television, and culture.

When it comes to academic help for teens, parents can be particularly frustrated. "I can't help my kid write a term paper and I certainly can't help with chemistry or algebra!" That's probably true, and even if you could, you should not provide that sort of assistance. But there are two important things that parents can do. First, they can insist that their teens keep an assignment notebook and calendar, and parents can check this every day. Personal organization is one of the most important factors that distinguishes successful high school students. Second, parents can insist that their children engage in regular writing. Writing, particularly nonfiction writing with editing and rewriting, is strongly associated with improved student achievement in every other academic area, including math, science, and social studies. Here are three things parents can do to improve student writing:

1. Thank-you notes. That's right – old-fashioned, handwritten thank-you notes. Sending thank-you notes is not just good manners, but will distinguish your children from the vast majority who never take the time to extend this simple courtesy.

2. Family history. The next time you visit grandparents or other older relatives, ask your teens to take some time to interview them, asking them about their parents and grandparents and the times they remember. The World War II generation is vanishing, and if you are lucky enough to have relatives who experienced that era, have your teens write about it. It may rekindle an interest in history and, at the very least, will renew relationships in your family. You probably have family

members who remember the Civil Rights movement or the Vietnam era. Have your teens write about those memories. This will be more compelling than anything they have heard in class or read in a textbook.

3. Advice to new students. Ask your teens to write to a younger sibling or family friend of elementary school or middle school age. Give them advice on what is required for success in high school. Their definition of "success" should include not only academic success, but safety, social relationships, and other things that they wish they had known before they entered high school.

Finally, there are things that parents can do to help the entire school. If your school doesn't have a newspaper, help to start one. I volunteer in one of my children's school every week and we publish a newspaper full of student writing, including news stories, sports news, editorials, cartoons, puzzles, advice columns, and anything else that interests the students. The students run the show, editing, writing, and distributing the newspaper. The newspaper staff includes learning-disabled students who have made important contributions and work with other colleagues on the newspaper staff to express their opinions and contribute to the paper in meaningful ways.

52 **I encourage my students to turn in a rough draft of any papers I assign so that I can review them and make suggestions for improvement. I am finding it increasingly difficult to get students to revise their rough drafts when I give them back. The general attitude now is, 'I did it once, why do I have to do it again?' I have done this quite a bit over the years and I used to see improvement by the end of the school year. Not anymore. Any suggestions?**

I have experienced the same problem, with students from 2nd grade to 55-year-old graduate students. "I've already done that!" they all complain, sometimes with a remarkably similar tone of voice. I've dealt with this challenge in a couple of ways. For older students I use a point system that makes it clear that the rough draft is a separate and distinct assignment. Typically, for a 100 point assignment, I assign 50 points for the draft and 50 points for the final. Even the best rough draft gets a maximum of 50 points. The scoring rubric for the final draft makes clear that it should respect the feedback and contain clear improvements. For younger students, I simply appeal to the "Grandma" effect. We only put perfect work on the wall (or in the student newspaper or other public displays). Now, I know this is pretty good, but if Grandma is going to see it, we want it to be perfect. What can you do to make it even better? In brief, whether it's a doctoral dissertation or a review of *Mr. Popper's Penguins*, whether it's a writer many grades above grade level or a writer who is struggling and discouraged, I know that the best thing I can do as a teacher is to challenge my students to do better than they think they could do. I never—not once—help them by settling for a first draft.

53   **I'm currently working with my teachers on revising their current rubric and taking them through the writing process (what teachers will be doing within the content and what students will be doing). But I'm meeting with resistance and I have a question for you: Which is a stronger practice in writing: having students use the writing process or having students synthesize thinking in a written response (without formally using the writing process)?**

No question: they need to use the writing process. They need to brainstorm, make a graphic organizer, outline, rough draft, edit, feedback, and write a final draft (sometimes many final drafts). Remember, 66 percent of high school students get through school and never write a formal research paper. Then they go to technical school, community college, or university, and get hammered because they cannot write an essay or research paper. This is a basic life skill, and whether students are entering the world of work, technical school, or college, they need to be able to take ideas, organize them, and express them.

54 I would like to develop a writing rubric for my elementary school. I'd like it to end up prominently posted in all classrooms and in the hallways. The communications skills specialist and assistant principal thought it was an interesting idea, but not for the primary grades. They thought it had potential for grades 3, 4, and 5 only. What are your feelings on this?

  Should rubrics be used for later elementary grades only? I just returned from a very successful district that uses rubrics for everything from behavior to writing to math problem-solving in KINDERGARTEN. Parents in the room testified that their 1st graders could say, "I got a 3 on this one, but I know how to make it a 4." The rubrics, of course, are not in obscure academic language—indeed, the children helped to make them so the language was clear. To see a visual example of this, check out the *Video Journal of Education*, Volumes 802 and 803, where you will see footage of 2nd grade students creating a writing rubric. The language is inventive and meaningful to children of that age, and you could see that the children are totally engaged.

55 My school is looking at how to measure writing to show growth on a quarterly basis. What would your suggestion be? We would like to get away from using a 4, 3, 2, 1 score as the score may not show growth. For example, a student scores a low 2 on the rubric at the beginning of the 1st quarter, then a high 2 during the next quarter. How is the growth shown? Is this where a narrative is included explaining the score and what that means? How would you show growth in writing on a quarterly basis?

You are presuming that if we have more points—say, eight rather than four—then it is easier to "show growth." That may be true in the short run, but whatever you gain in the good feelings from this growth, you lose in reliability and consistency of scoring. In general the more points you have on a scale, the harder it is for teacher to agree on what a "3" or "6" or "12" really means. I'm an advocate of four points because it provides a meaningful distinction because there is a HUGE difference between "proficient" and "progressing." It also allows for consistency, because 80 percent of teachers can, with a good rubric, agree on what "proficient" really means.

So, back to the question of showing growth. The real measurement is the "Percentage of students proficient or higher." If you have someone move from a low 2 to a high 2, as you suggest, then the challenge remains to get the child to a 3, or proficient, score. We should not remove that incentive.

56 We are questioning our assessment process for writing. Presently, we give monthly writing prompts with each prompt being a different genre of writing (personal narrative/ persuasive writing). The prompts are not always based on/in content discipline (social studies/science). The question is: Should writing prompts be a consistent genre of writing (for the year per grade level) and always based on a content area? We are considering making it so that the students will be assessed monthly over the same type of nonfiction writing, with each grade level being responsible for a form of writing to ensure understanding (ex: 6th grade would do a research form, 5th grade persuasive, 4th grade personal narrative, etc.). What do you think?

First, I want to congratulate you and your faculty for the progress you have made and also for your commitment to doing a great deal of student writing and for undertaking the difficult task of collaborative scoring. You are doing the right thing, and your question indicates that you have already overcome the most important barriers. You are far, far ahead of the vast majority of schools that are still struggling with whether they should even consider monthly writing and collaborative scoring.

I understand the dilemma. How can we assess writing consistently when we are also considering subject matter and when we are changing the writing genre? Let me offer a couple of practical suggestions.

First, don't try to combine the scoring of content with written expression. If you want to use a science or social studies prompt, that's great. But give one score for content and a separate score for written expression. This allows teachers to say, "Your knowledge of history and geography is wonderful, but you still need to rewrite your paper." Or they might say, "Your written expression is really great, but you need a better grounding in the facts." The more specific the scoring guide, the better. Two different scores, one for content and one for writing, will help your students to focus on what you expect of them.

Second, the genres do change, but be careful about associating them with a single grade level. In my view, students in grades 3 through 6 should be able to write essays that:

- Persuade with evidence

- Describe with rigor

- Identify similarities and differences (compare and contrast)

The content and context may change, but the scoring rubric for written expression will not change.

Again, you are doing the right thing. My congratulations to you and your teachers for perseverance and hard work.

57 **I have heard you speak of research studies that were related to writing performance mitigating the impact of poverty. You also advocated a large literacy block with a focus on the writing process. Might you share with me those particular studies in full or refer me to the site where I might obtain them?**

There is a substantial amount of literature about the relationship between writing and student achievement. One of the most compelling examples of this was a National Science Foundation study documented in the Summer 2002 edition of the Bilingual Research Journal entitled, "Helping English learners increase achievement through inquiry-based science instruction." I have also published similar findings in:

- NASSP *Bulletin*, December 2000, "Standards are not enough."

- *Daily Disciplines of Leadership* (Jossey-Bass), 2002.

- *Accountability for Learning* (ASCD), 2004.

- *Reason to Write* (Simon & Schuster), 2002.

See also:

- Linda Darling-Hammond, *The Right to Learn* (Jossey-Bass, 1997)—in particular, in about the first 100 pages or so, numerous references to the relationship between authentic assessment, writing, and student achievement.

- Lucy McCormick Calkins, *The Art of Teaching Writing* (Heinemann).

I would never contend that these relationships are perfect. There are examples where lots of writing takes place and there are inadequate gains in achievement, and no doubt examples of where gains occur without increases in writing. Nevertheless, the relationships I cited are strong and persistent, bridging disciplines, grade levels, and geographic areas. I was challenged by a graduate student who said that the relationships were "too good"—that is, that they were measuring the same variable. I think that she was correct—the reason for the strong relationship between writing as I have defined it (nonfiction writing, with editing and rewriting) and student achievement in other academic disciplines, is the relationship to thinking, reasoning, and analysis, not merely the skill of writing.

Finally, even acknowledging the inevitable weaknesses of any correlative research, we must ask, "What is the alternative?" Unfortunately, the alternative I see too frequently is mindless test prep masquerading as academic preparation. I'm attempting to make the classic Educational Testing Service argument—that test performance is not a function of test prep, but of thinking, reasoning, and analysis. When writing is done well, along with editing and rewriting, students and teachers can promote the reasoning skills that we endorse.

Show Me the Proof

58   **What articles and books would you recommend that I use with building principals to make the case for the implementation of a nonfiction, across-the-curriculum writing program? I would prefer to show my principals the value of such a program through research.**

With regard to research, let me offer several sources, ranging from free downloads from our web site to more extensive published sources.

Start with www.MakingStandardsWork.com. On the "Resources" part of the web site you'll find many examples, case studies, and research citations regarding writing.

Next, consider my article "Standards are not enough" published in the NASSP *Bulletin*, December 2000. It is a good orientation to the research on writing. For leaders, I would consider the book *The Daily Disciplines of Leadership* along with *The Leader's*

Guide to Standards. There you will find original regression coefficients and scattergrams. In addition, consider *Accountability in Action* as a source with research and case studies on this issue. Of course, it's important that principals consider research from different perspectives. I already cited the National Science Foundation Report in the presentation this week. You might also want to consider Linda Darling-Hammond's classic *The Right to Learn*—see particularly the first 100 pages for evidentiary links between performance assessment, including writing, and student performance on content-based tests. Also, see Lucy Calkins' terrific book, *The Art of Teaching Writing*. One of the later chapters focuses on the link between writing and content courses. Finally—and this is a superior book—look at Mel Levine's newest work, *The Myth of Laziness*. He has case studies with students of every conceivable description and particularly emphasizes the importance of writing.

59 **I would like to see research & citations for the data regarding achievement and nonfiction writing. I need that research and those sources. It is crucial to a 6-district in service we're holding soon. I appreciate any help you can give me.**

I am happy to help. The following sources are a partial list of the abundant literature on the connection between writing and student achievement:

- Reeves, Douglas (2002). *The Daily Disciplines of Leadership* (Jossey-Bass).

- Allen, Rick (2003, Summer). "Expanding Writing's Role in Learning" ASCD *Curriculum Update*.

- Reeves, Douglas (2000, December). "Standards are not enough," NASSP *Bulletin*.

- Darling-Hammond, Linda (1997). *The Right to Learn* (Jossey-Bass).

- Graham, Steve, et al, (2003, June). "Primary grade teachers' instructional adaptations for struggling writers: A national survey," *Journal of Educational Psychology*, vol 95, no 2, pp. 279+.

- Calkins, Lucy (1996). *The Art of Teaching Writing*. (Heinnemann).

- Reeves, Douglas (2002). *Reason to Write*. Simon & Schuster.

- Reeves, Douglas (2004). *Accountability for Learning*. ASCD.

This is a partial list. There is a pretty substantial amount of evidence on this point. I also have new publications coming out this year with some 2003 research studies. You can also refer your staff to our web site for several free downloads of research, along with past issues of *Focus on Achievement* that include case studies of effective practice.

Of course, there is nothing magic about writing. It is representative of a mix of many other things, including thinking, analysis, reasoning, and when done property, clearly articulated expectations and consistent feedback from teachers. My experience is that this is much more difficult than the typical reading program. It shouldn't be either/or: Learning decoding skills doesn't help kids with reading comprehension; writing alone without decoding skills doesn't make much sense either. That's why the successful schools we work with typically spend 2 1/2 to 3 hours every day on literacy, with about 2 hours on reading and 1 hour on writing.

I understand the need for scientifically-based research, but we need to be careful about the application of the term. Would we ask for statistical evidence to say that reading is a good idea in science, social studies, and math? While I think the evidence to support writing in the content areas is very, very strong, I also want to be careful about the proposition that even the most common sense educational practices, such as reading and writing, are regarded as ineffective unless scientific research establishes their validity.

Classroom Issues

Classroom Issues

60   I am wondering if you can point me toward research that supports the importance of looping at the high school level. I am working to foster the importance of relationships as connected to learning by keeping kids with teachers for two years within particular classes.

I'm not aware of large-scale research at the secondary level. I do know of case studies in which teachers report that, as a result of looping, they know their students better, spend September and October really teaching rather than getting to know students, and most importantly, that when they have multi-year looping and maintain multi-year portfolios, teachers can see exceptional evidence of progress in student work over the years. That's not statistical evidence, but it is common sense, and sometimes that's even better.

What you may wish to consider is this: do a pilot project (I elaborate on this idea in the book *Making Standards Work*). Have two or three teachers try it for two years and then report results to the entire faculty. Base your ultimate decision on your own internal findings and the evidence with your own students.

61   I have heard you mention the concept of a 'welcome center' for new students. Our school has a large amount of student mobility and I am looking for ways to cope with it. Can you give me any ideas?

The "welcome center" idea came from districts in Pennsylvania and Indiana that had very high mobility rates and lots of new students coming in, including those who had moved from neighboring districts and those who came from foreign countries. Hardly any of them had student records. Under the leadership of the library media center specialist, they created a "welcome center" that was the first stop for every new student. Students spend from one to three days there before assignment to a classroom.

Each student received a reading and writing assessment. This was based on the recent "Information Literacy Standards" that makes it clear that we have important resources in our library media professionals, who are experts in literacy and who, frankly, are underused professional resources in many schools.

Students typically find the library media center a welcoming place, and they can almost always find books, videos, or audio material that is appropriate for them. In one case, the media center staff enlisted parents to help provide appropriate native language material (Polish, Russian, Puntonghua, Hmung) so each student could find something that was appropriate on their first day in school. By the end of the day (or two or three), the child has a new folder, a reading level and writing sample, and some insightful observations on learning needs and student interests that were noted by the library media center specialist. It is a golden gift to the busy classroom teacher.

"Veteran" students in the school also took a leadership role in the welcome center, with a "nobody eats alone" rule. 5th grade students would go to the media center, pick up new students, escort them to the cafeteria, show them around the school, and make them feel welcome and befriended.

All of this is a remarkable contrast to having a child sit in a busy principal's office, quickly assigned to an unfamiliar classroom, and given to a teacher who has no idea of the child's background and learning needs.

62 **The practice at my building has been to test students at the 5th and 6th grade level and ability group them for math in groups such as low 5th grade math, regular 5th grade math, 6th grade math and 7th grade math. I have found some research that supports not grouping low students for instruction in academic areas. I believe that you have stated that students should be taught at their grade level and the time altered to meet their needs. Should all of the low students be put together and be taught at a slow pace or do the students benefit from their**

peers that are more successful at math? Is there some research I can present to my teachers to show them that we should not put all of the low students together or should we continue this practice?

We agree that students should be taught "on grade level" but, as a former math teacher, I also empathize with your colleagues' concern that students who lack basic skills will only be frustrated and angry if we fail to give them basic instruction before we give them advanced challenges. I have personally struggled with this issue. In middle school, I had immigrant students who had great math skills, but poor English skills, and I had native kids with pretty good English skills, and lousy math skills. So "grouping" became a more complex matter than just a score. I faced the same problem with graduate students, where I had high school math teachers sitting next to preschool teachers, who were next to nursing students, who were next to epidemiological researchers, all the same stat class! I then had to admit that what I faced was no more complex than what most middle school math teachers face every day. So, whatever it's worth, here is my solution.

The alternative is not either "low math" or "regular math," but rather that we provide intensive intervention for students who need it. If, for example, I am a 6th grade student who can't multiply, it's really hard to expect me to do exponents. That doesn't mean that I ignore exponents and just do multiplication facts, but it DOES mean that I must have the time to do both, and that means more than a forty-five minute math period each day. The same applies if I had a 6th grader reading on a 3rd grade level. Don't ask me to assign a novel to a student who can't sound out words. Give me more TIME. That will mean, particularly for the 5th and 6th grader, that I can't do every subject, every elective, every special area, and continue to pretend that every academic area deserves equal time. Literacy and math are essential, and kids cannot enter high school with success and confidence unless they can read on grade level and perform high school level mathematics.

I work with schools that give three hours to literacy and ninety minutes to two hours every DAY in math. If we fail to do so, then the students are at risk for dropping out later in school, along with a lifetime of consequences.

So, the bottom line is, I agree that kids need grade level instruction. But they ALSO need the foundations, and that takes more time.

63 **We are being told to teach at grade level no matter what the students' abilities are. We have many 8th grade students with 6th grade-level math and reading skills, yet we are told not to teach to their current level, but rather teach to their grade level. May I have your opinion on this?**

It's not "either/or" but "both/and." As a math teacher, I did get my students to exponents, just as I would get an 8th grader to chart linear (y=mx+b) graphs and nonlinear exponential graphs. But I could never have done that if I didn't also take extra time to ensure that they could multiply. So, yes, I did "grade-level" work and believe very much in that concept. But if my student is several grades below where he needs to be, I must have the time to catch up. To be specific, I know of schools that spend three hours each day on literacy—two hours reading and one hour writing; and 90 to 120 minutes on math. That means that some other things give way. But it's the only way we can get our students to a level of proficiency that is necessary.

Finally, do not try to have them proficient at EVERYTHING. Rather, consider the "Power Standards" approach in which you and your colleagues identify which standards (typically about twelve per grade per subject) are the most important for the next level of instruction. That will save a lot of time and keep your curriculum and classroom assessment focused in the right areas.

64 When discussing mixed ability grouping, you outline the benefits of a standards-based education both for students performing at high level and a low level of proficiency. But in the classroom, what happens to the middle-level students? How do teachers challenge and engage the students who demonstrate proficiency after a few tries, therefore not needing assistance from their peers, but also not strong enough (or willing, for that matter) to teach others? I assume the answer to my question lies somewhere in between the approaches for low and high level performers, but I was curious how it really played out in the real world.

This is why we encourage multitask assessments, with the rule of thumb including four tasks. Some kids might zoom through the first three tasks and be slowed down on the fourth, while other kids need help completing the second task. Moreover, the zoomers in math might be the ones needing extra time in a different subject. There are no generic low, middle, and high performers; it's just a question of achieving proficiency. Of course some kids, the zoomers, may meet the standard quickly, and a good multitask performance assessment will challenge them to go way beyond the standard. But that provides good classroom management and, most importantly, time: time for the teacher to provide tutoring, help, and assistance for other students to achieve proficiency. Note that the zoomers don't just do "more work" ("You did five pages, now do seven"). Rather, they do work that is qualitatively different in engagement and sophistication. See the "Ideal School" exercise in the back of *Making Standards Work* for an example.

65   I am the AP of a middle school, and our district has been implementing differentiated instruction for the past two years. Most of our staff is using differentiated lessons, but we are getting questions about assessing the different groups in the classroom. The one question which keeps coming up is, "How do I justify the grades for groups which are doing easier work?" If you could give some suggestions or ideas that I can share with my staff, I would appreciate it.

Let me begin by suggesting that you can use a "Standards Achievement Report" to clearly communicate to parents and students what a child has done and what she has not yet accomplished. If, for whatever local reason, you have to use letter grades and award someone a "B," you still have the obligation to say, "Marcus has achieved these four standards, he is making progress on these eight standards, and has not begun to master these thirteen standards." In clear and convincing language, tell the student and parent what the student can and cannot do.

You can find details of the Standards Achievement Report in the book *Making Standards Work*.

66   I am an ESL teacher for K-5. We are moving to inclusion rather than pullout, although we still pull out for newcomers to the U.S. for their first year and give intensive English instruction. Please direct me to the research and methodology that is employed by the 90/90/90 schools, or any information relevant to teaching second language learners. I am wondering if there is a specific standard that must be reached before the student benefits more from inclusion than pullout.

Thanks very much for your very thoughtful question. The central challenge with ESL students is that they are not a homogeneous group. We can have three students all called

"ESL" and the first one is literate in a home language using the same letters and most of the same letter sounds as English, the second one is literate in a home language, but the alphabet is Putonghua or Cyrillic, and the third student is not literate in any language, either English or the home language. All three are called "ESL" but all three require very different instructional strategies.

Here are some common guidelines to consider:

1. Conduct pre-assessments and very frequent (at least monthly) follow-up assessments. The old saying that "it takes seven years" is just as ridiculous as the contention that "with immersion they all get it in one year." Students have differences that must be identified and applied to instructional strategies.

2. Focus the curriculum overwhelmingly on literacy: three hours a day is not excessive. But the curriculum must not be exclusively related to literacy. I have taught immigrant children who LOVE math class because they are more at home with numbers, shapes, and mathematical concepts than words. Indeed, their love of math provided a nice bridge to build their English skills.

3. Engage in early and frequent writing. The philosophy that language development is "speak, read, then write" is wrong. Language development is holistic, and students very new to the English language (and to your school) can engage in writing, although with fragmentary words and sentences. Associating writing with pictures (both externally generated and created by students) as well as interactive journals with teachers is a sound practice. Writing is also an emotionally safe method of expression for older ESL students.

4. Include opportunities for students to engage in music, art, PE, technology, home languages, or other languages. Although English language literacy is the first priority in the curriculum, these curriculum areas provide opportunities for students to shine and become engaged (and avoid discouragement) in school.

There is, as you know, a very rich literature on ESL teaching techniques. These ideas are just a start for you to consider.

67 **Are there effective resources or best practices in the area of writing to deal with a significantly large ESL population?**

The books *Reason to Write* and the *Reason to Write Student Handbook* provide more elaboration, but in general, the keys for ESL students include multiple opportunities for success, multiple ways of representing ideas (writing, oral, webs, pictures), and focused feedback. By "focused feedback" I mean don't try to do grammar, organization, word choice, simile, metaphor, irony, and spelling all at the same time. With my ESL students, I would start focusing on JUST organization— beginning, middle, and end. If we had that, it was worthy of celebration. Then I might add just ONE convention, such as capitalization or ending punctuation. Incremental steps, regular feedback, and opportunities for IMMEDIATE correction and success are the keys.

68 **I need some research and information on the increased achievement for non-severely disabled special education students in a standards-based environment. Can you assist me with this?**

I just returned from working with the Sanders School in Indianapolis. They work with students with Individualized Education Plans and had more than 50 percent meet state standards on the latest test and have displayed significant improvements in other academic areas as well. This is consistent with similar situations in Aspen and Milwaukee where a high percentage of IEP students succeeded on state tests. I've noticed some common characteristics among these schools.

First, they are consistent with accommodations and adaptations. They do not only use these during test week, but are consistent throughout the year. Students are thus far less traumatized when the test is consistent with their previous classroom experiences.

Second, they place an extraordinary emphasis on writing. Sanders has particularly strong evidence of the impact of multiple (nine or ten) drafts and precise feedback that is associated with dramatic improvements in student writing.

You might want to conduct an Educational Resources Information Center (ERIC) search at http://eric.ed.gov/ for additional large scale research on this point.

69 **We are revamping our 3rd, 4th, and 5th grade after-school remedial program in an attempt to raise scores on our state test. We have many 3rd graders who did not pass the test who will retake it in the spring as 4th graders. We have many 5th graders who did not pass it in the 3rd or 4th grade.**

Where should we start the benchmark? The teachers will need to know where to begin with the students because many children will not be with their daily teacher for the extra help.

Monitoring the students' progress is a must. There will be so many different levels and needs, I am not sure where to begin. I want success for the students to improve our overall scores. Can you help?

You identified the most important issue when you said that you needed to identify the individual needs of each student.

I would recommend that you create an "Individualized Learning Plan" for each student. Rather than just last year's test score, it should identify the SPECIFIC SKILLS that the students need to succeed on the state test. Then the students should be assessed on EACH SKILL. You can use local resources provided by your central office or your own home-grown skill assessments, but these students must be assessed throughout the year—even as often as once per week—to identify the specific skill level of students.

The Individualized Learning Plan will show where the teacher must concentrate for each student. Some after school programs just repeat the same mistake made in the classroom: moving every child through a curriculum at the same pace, whether or not the child is learning the material. If the 4th grader is struggling with addition, then stop the multiplication and division lessons and build basic skills first. If she is struggling with consonant blends, then stop the geography lessons and go back and teach her to read.

The previous year's state test scores are a starting point, but they are not a substitute for identifying the specific skill development needs of each child and then working intensively on each of those skills between now and the spring.

70 **I have two classes of 6th grade language arts/social studies in a block schedule, which I love. My classes are typical because they have students who can and will, and students who can and won't, and students who are working to their ability, but their ability level is low. How many opportunities do I give to students to meet the standard before moving on to the next standard? Some standards in language arts can be ongoing, but in social studies, our time for the standards covering Egypt, Kush, and Mesopotamia is only about three to four weeks. An 'inch wide and a mile deep' is a great idea, but at some point, the classes need to move forward, perhaps leaving some students behind. What are your thoughts?**

Your question is one of the most important ones in the entire field of standards. The essence of standards-based education is that we maintain a fixed standard and allow time to be the variable. But the practical question becomes, "How much time is sufficient?"

In practice, it is more that most people think and less than the prophets of doom think. Some teachers take a "one shot and you're done" approach, which is more likely to measure what students learned before they walked into the class rather than what they learned in school. Multiple opportunities for success provide greater respect for teacher feedback, because teacher feedback on assessments must be understood and respected in order for students to make progress. In the "multiple opportunities" model, the penalty for poor work is not a low grade, but more work—more "opportunities"—and I know a lot of middle school students who are not very motivated by grades, but who are VERY motivated by the prospect of avoiding additional work. Lucy Calkins, founder of the Literacy Project at Columbia University, routinely expects to have students provide seven, eight, or nine drafts of their work before it is finished.

But what about the other extreme: the defiant student? Does the term "multiple opportunities" mean "infinite opportunities"? No. It is reasonable to set a cutoff every few weeks and give students the stark choice: become proficient or risk failure. Do not reward poor performance with a C or a D, but tell students the truth: non-proficient performance receives no credit. While this may seem drastic (basically an A, B, C or F grading system), it does get results. Some students (those who can but won't, as you say) will test you, call your bluff, and dare you to fail them. As long as you have a safety-net mechanism (typically two weeks after a failure, students can redeem themselves), then charge ahead and do it.

If you take this advice, two things will happen. First, the quality of student work will improve. Second, the quantity of student complaints (and perhaps a few parent complaints as well) will increase. In the words of one student I interviewed who suffered under an A, B, C, and F system, "Hey, man, this SUCKS. I used to be able to get stuff done and get a D, but they don't give D's any more. And it's such a hassle to get a C, you might as well get a B." This gives us the splendid spectacle of a whining adolescent bellyaching all the way to the honor roll. As a former middle school teacher myself, I can only smile. Some still stop me years later and thank me. My job wasn't to be popular, but to have my students be successful.

So, set your standards. Give them multiple opportunities for success. But if they persist in willful failure, call it what it is: willful failure, not tolerated, condoned, and accepted failure.

71　I am principal of a public high school where my predecessor resigned because she was asked to implement honors classes at the 9th and 10th grade levels, which she objected to as a return to tracking. I don't want to see a return to rigid tracking either. However, I'm not sure that there isn't a small percentage of kids who are so advanced in their academic skills that they need something different.

Many of my progressive friends believe that tracking is bad, but few can really explain how we can have 10th graders in the same class who read from 3rd grade to 12th grade level and not have someone's needs not addressed. I'm actually most worried that the teenager who reads like the 3rd grader is the one who gets left behind. It seems meeting standards means groupings have to be different sometimes, and we just need to make sure boundaries are fluid and not hard. What are your thoughts on this subject?

Thanks very much for your very thoughtful inquiry. Tracking is an emotional issue and, as a result, many people seem unwilling to address it rationally. First, let's consider the realities:

Every school has tracking; the only issue is whether it is explicit or hidden. Hidden tracking happens particularly in those schools that proudly proclaim that "we never do tracking," yet some kids succeed, others don't, and after the 9th grade year, students make strikingly different choices about their academic careers. Even with the same classes, expectations about what is regarded as acceptable can vary widely from one student to another, but huge numbers of students get by with C's and D's when they are not proficient. To stop and give them extra time and extra assistance so that they would have an opportunity for future success might look like tracking, so these students in desperate need fall through the cracks and never get the opportunity they deserve. Just as bad is the case of the students who came to high school in need of challenge to keep them engaged, and the "factory classes" with students, as you suggest, with reading levels from 3rd to 12th grade, quickly send the message that this is not a place of challenge or engagement. At best, these students zone out and pass. At worst, they become disruptive, develop discipline problems, or find something else that will excite them—drugs, unhealthy relationships, etc.

Therefore, the question is not whether or not to have tracking—we always have it—but whether the tracking is permanent or temporary. Permanent tracking is the reason most of your friends hate it. It's redolent of the "bluebirds, robins, and blackbirds" of our childhood, with choices of color no accident. The kids get those labels early in school, and they stick.

What I advocate is an opportunity for DE-TRACKING—giving students intensive intervention so that they have the opportunity to succeed later on. In the short term, that means that some students will need extra time and extra help, while other students will need challenge and enrichment. But ALL students get what they need when they need it, not after they are in trouble.

I think honors classes in 9th and 10th grade are fine, provided that you meet two conditions:

1. The classes really are significantly different in curriculum and assessment, perhaps linked to AP tests or an International Baccalaureate curriculum. They cannot be a disguised way to separate kids based on appearance.

2. The district creates a mechanism in middle school for ALL students to have the OPPORTUNITY (but not the obligation) to take those honors classes. This is the huge equity issue that bothers your friends. The honors classes will be segregated by race and class unless you take explicit steps to create an opportunity for all students to take them. You may also need to have the faculty members who offer the honors classes agree to provide assistance and intervention to students who take the class and who are struggling. You can't have honors classes only for those students who have a strong academic support structure at home, with parents who will hire tutors and check homework. The classes must

be open to all, and provisions must be made for success for all students.

The bottom line is, you don't achieve equity by pretending that there is no tracking or failing to provide opportunities for challenge and enrichment such as honors classes. You achieve equity by ensuring that EVERY student has the opportunity to take honors classes, and a support structure so that students who a year ago did not think of themselves as "honors students" will be willing to take those challenging classes and succeed.

72 Can you please help me to locate research that shows the link between achievement and increased self-esteem?

The most recent research on the self-esteem / self-concept / self-efficacy / student achievement connections can be found in the March 2003 issue of the *Journal of Educational Psychology*, in an article by Guay, Marsh, and Boivin entitled, "Academic Self-Concept and Academic Achievement: Developmental Perspectives on Their Causal Ordering." Of course, there are many studies on this subject, and a good synthesis of this research can be found in the text *Educational Psychology* by Robert Slavin.

Do remember that there are stronger psychological variables than self-esteem. In particular, a feeling of personal efficacy ("I know that my work makes a difference" and "I know that when I plan and work it influences the outcome") is more powerful than merely a feeling of self-esteem. In particular, beware of people who claim that self esteem is an externally induced variable— that teachers "create" high self esteem by what they say to children. That's part of it, but a bigger part is students gaining genuine self-esteem through a confidence that they really are competent.

73 I'm looking for information on attendance issues in the classroom. We want to use this to present to parents with elementary children who have started to show troubling patterns of attendance. Do you know of a 'critical' number of absences that begins to impact achievement?

There is a very revealing study on this subject from the New York State Department of Education, which was cited in *Education Week's* October 18, 2000 issue. The title of the article is, "As Studies Stress Link to Scores, Districts Get Tough on Attendance" and was written by Robert C. Johnston. The New York study said that when absences exceeded 15 percent of school days, the probability of student dropout or failure rose dramatically—no real news to any teacher or administrator. Specifically, students with an 85 percent attendance rates scored below the 54th percentile on state tests. The important implication, however, is that we need to focus on non-attenders who are "in the bubble." That is, the difference between 90 percent and 85 percent attendance is far more critical than the difference between 98 percent and 93 percent, or 55 percent and 50 percent.

74 I have trouble getting K–5 teachers to understand the reason for homework, and more importantly, the reason for NO HOMEWORK. Please help me with some examples or articles to support the real reasons for homework or a lack thereof.

The best contemporary data source for this question is Robert Marzano's splendid book, *What Works in Schools*, published by the ASCD in 2003. Briefly, homework IS important and helpful IF it meets these criteria:

1. It is used to reinforce skills, not to introduce new concepts.

2. It receives IMMEDIATE feedback for improved performance

3. Teachers acknowledge valid attempts and engagement in the assignment, not merely the right answer.

With regard to the people who say that today's homework is unprecedented and too much, I would refer them to the article entitled "A Crime Against Children: The Scourge of Homework in Our Schools." The date is 1900 in *Ladies Home Journal*. Somewhere, I think, there was a Cro-Magnon student complaining about too much homework. Clearly, I'm not defending mindless and unhelpful homework. But students DO need to learn the time management and organization skills that homework builds. Fifteen to twenty minutes in grades 2-3; thirty minutes in grades 4-5, an hour in middle school, and two hours in high school are reasonable requirements. If, of course, kids fail to organize their time, they wind up with the typical complaint of "ten hours of homework!" That usually means one hour of homework, accumulated over ten days. Teachers therefore must not only teach academic skills, but time management and organization skills as well. That will give them a lifelong skill to use in college, technical school, graduate school, and life.

Grading and Reporting Data

Grading for Fairness and Accuracy

 75 At our elementary school, the policy on math problems is to take off 2 points per problem if students don't include the "label." This means if the student doesn't write the word "tickets" in a problem asking how many tickets were sold, they are docked two points. Their grade can go from a passing grade to a failing one if they don't label all the problems. The teachers do not, however, give partial credit for including the "label" if the student gets the math wrong but writes the label correctly. They say that taking off for the labels is an important part of "following directions," but our report cards have a separate conduct grade for "listens and follows directions." What are your thoughts on this?

As a math teacher myself, I understand the quandary. We want students to know the math and also to understand the context of the problem. I used to tell my students, whether they were in elementary school or graduate school, "Mathematics is about describing the universe using numbers, symbols, and words, and we're going to use all three of those this year." I tried to make it clear that is about communication, not just about calculation, and it sounds as if your math teachers have similar feelings.

Now to the grading issue. I love your idea of distinguishing between academic content and "listening and following directions," but we would all acknowledge that on a test and in life, students must do BOTH. It's not an either/or proposition. Therefore, the report card is a great idea and the math teacher who insists that students label their problems have a great idea. I don't even mind if they take points off. HOWEVER, those deductions should be in PENCIL, and the student should, prior to turning work in, conduct a self-assessment. In some cases, I have seen a checklist by the teacher's desk and in other cases (including all of my classes) there was a checklist on top of the test that the student had to complete. It included things such as

"Name on paper" and could also include "Labels on each answer." If a student still fails to label the answer correctly, the appropriate response is not a failing grade, but the requirement that the student do it again (that's why the deduction should be in pencil). The lesson I want them to learn is not, "I'm a failure in math" but rather, "I'd better label my answers or it's a lot of extra work so I might as well do it right the first time." When the student answers the problem correctly, the deduction can be removed. It's the BEHAVIOR of labeling the problem that I want to reinforce, and my experience suggests that in some cases, it takes more than one-trial learning for that to take place.

76 **I have heard it said that averaging a student's grade with a zero in it for missing work is somewhat harsh, because they have such a deficit to come up from. It seems that if a 50 were assigned to an F it would be easier to bring that grade up, or perhaps a fairer place to start in the averaging process. Should missing assignments still get zeros since nothing was turned in, or should they be assigned an F with a standard percentage so the student is not so far down in the hole that he can't get out?**

I do believe that teachers should emphasize timeliness and responsibility. However, there are better ways to do this than awarding a "zero" for late or absent student work.

First, the "zero" is mathematically inaccurate. Accuracy demands that the interval between each grade—A, B, C, D, and F—is equal. When an A is a 90, and the B, C, and D are 80, 70, and 60, respectively, then the next lower grade—the F—should be 50, not zero. To make an F a zero is to state that failing to hand in work is SIX TIMES WORSE than handing in work that is of D quality. I have never heard a teacher make the argument than an F is six times worse than a D.

Second and more importantly, the purpose of grading and assessment is to improve student work—not merely to render an evaluation. Therefore, the best "punishment" for late or absent work is not a low grade, but additional work. I know many students, particularly teenagers, who are not motivated by a low grade, but are very motivated by the prospect of more work, or (more positively) the prospect of avoiding work by turning in high quality work the first time.

In general, we need to use grades less for punishment and more for the development of better student work habits and higher-quality work.

77 **I have heard you speak of the inconsistency in using the 4 point GPA and the 100 percent scale as measures. I am not able to explain this to a fellow teacher. Could you help me with this?**

Thanks very much for your question. Essentially, it is the difference between an interval and non-interval scale. If we graded students on an A, B, C, D, F scale with the corresponding numbers 4, 3, 2, 1, and zero, then we would have an interval scale; that is, a 1 point interval between each rating. But if, for purely arbitrary and traditional reasons, we change from that 4, 3, 2, 1, 0 scale to 90, 80, 70, 60, 0 scale, then we are suddenly saying that the F is SIX TIMES WORSE than the D. This is not true. It is an interval error. The "zero" which happens due to lost homework or poor test performance is, indeed, a bad thing, but is it really six times worse than the student who received a D?

I'm not excusing bad behavior by students, but I insist that bad behavior, whether it is absent homework or poor test performance, is measured accurately, and not as something that is six times as bad as a merely wretched D performance.

78 **My school is interested in introducing and eventually establishing a 'No Failure Policy' that allows students to reach mastery level in all subject levels. As we begin this process, it would be extremely helpful if you could provide us with examples of high schools currently utilizing this approach.**

You should take a look at the "No D" policy: Students must earn at least a "C" in order to receive credit. The example I know best is Juneau Douglas High School in Alaska, but in fact several high schools have been featured in *Education Week* (see www.edweek.org) doing the same thing. Their point is that we engage in "surprise" grading when we tell students that they are proficient by giving them passing grades, and then have them take a high school exit exam which they are doomed to fail because we failed to insist on real proficiency in the classroom.

The other context in which you might have heard the "no fail" is the 90/90/90 research in which the consequence of failure on classroom assessments is "multiple opportunities for success" rather than a failing grade. I don't want to imply, however, that this means "infinite opportunities" or "no possibility of failure." But we can substantially REDUCE the number of failures by providing more time, more opportunities, and more teaching.

However, this is a subject on which the experience of other districts, even in the most rigorously controlled studies, will not address the concerns of people who are wedded to a traditional grading structure. Rather than focusing on the D itself, this would be a good opportunity to step back and ask:

1. What are the fundamental purposes of our assessment and grading policies? (I would hope that the answer would be something about improving student achievement and the professional practices of teachers, but that is a discussion worth having.)

2. What is the most effective way to communicate student performance to students and parents? How is this "most effective way" similar to or different from our current report card practices?

3. If our students meet the academic standards of the state, school, and district, what grade will they receive? Is this answer the same for every teacher?

4. Does a "passing grade" (anything above an F) mean that the student has been successful in the course, has met state standards, and is ready for the next level of instruction?

5. Does our grading system allow for early intervention and improvement of student achievement based on the feedback from the teacher? Or is the feedback, in the form of a grade, too late in the case of D and F students so that the grade functions only as a report of failure rather than a device for improvement?

6. To what extent does our present grading system lead to reflections that improve professional practices? For example, are there case studies among faculty members in which a high number of low grades was followed by a change in professional practices and subsequent improvement in student performance?

In other words, the conversation is not about the D itself as a grade, but about the meaning of grades in general. I would particularly commend to you Tom Guskey's writings on this subject, including the terrific book he wrote with Jane Bailey entitled *Developing Grading and Reporting Systems for Student Learning*. (Corwin Press, 2001). In this book, they address several grading issues, including the inappropriate use of the zero and the incorrect use of the average. It is the accumulation of all of these issues, not just a discussion about the single letter. Finally, while Guskey provides a great deal of national research on grading, the real issues for your school will be the answers to the questions I have posed above. Grading is, to parents and students (and more than a few faculty!), almost an article of faith and an artifact of culture, not a decision influenced solely be evidence. Therefore, having open and honest conversations about the purposes of grading will help lead you to a decision that is fair and consistent with your values

Reporting Data to Reflect
Student Achievement

79 We have a standards-based report card that measures students' progress against an end-of-the-year expectation. One of the problems we struggle with is showing progress for the earlier grading periods. A '2' for 'Progressing Toward End-of-Year Standard' could mean that the student does not yet have the skills or understanding expected by the end of the year OR it could mean that part of the standard has not yet been taught. How do we address end-of-year vs. current progress?

This is a subject on which reasonable people of good will can differ, so let me offer my ideas, accepting that you and your colleagues may disagree. I favor using end-of-year expectations for what "proficient" should be. This means that the vast majority (but not all) students will be only "progressing" in October, because they have not yet had the instruction and background necessary to be proficient. My reasoning is twofold.

First, the price of progress in the spring is honesty in the fall. We need to tell the students and parents that their 4th graders have not yet, in the fall of their 4th grade year, met the standards. They need to work, read, write, do math, and learn. If we want to motivate students and teachers, we must show steady progress. "Only 18 percent of our students were proficient in October, but that percentage rose to 40 percent in December and we're on track to be at 100 percent by May." The essence of standards-based education is that all students will achieve standards, but not all on the same day. We should anticipate some variation here, and be happy that we have progress throughout the year.

Second, we need to challenge students to come to school already proficient. This is particularly true when students are above the national average and the primary enemy of student progress becomes complacency. Another important part of standards is not merely encouraging the discouraged student, but challenging the complacent student. "Okay, you came here proficient, so now what can we do to challenge you to achieve a level of exemplary performance?" For these students, standards are a floor, not a ceiling. These students are not motivated by letter grades and the continuing steady stream of A's, but they might be motivated by a standards-based report that says, "You're really doing fine—in fact, you are proficient far earlier than you need to be—but you are NOT yet exemplary and you've got some work to do."

My final point has to do with faculty motivation. If you just call "proficient" where you think students should be throughout the year, then it is very difficult if not impossible to show progress during the year. The percentage of students "meeting expectations" will be quite similar all year long. If, by contrast, you show "percentage of students meeting standards," then you can show steady and significant progress throughout the year.

80   I need some clarification. If I am going to look at a cohort over the past four years of testing, my understanding is that I should only look at those students who have remained in our schools for the past four years.

For example, if the 2nd grade enrollment is 250 students, the 3rd grade enrollment 225, the 4th grade enrollment 250, and the 5th grade enrollment 250, then the cohort for all four years should be the 150 students that have remained with us for the whole four years.

The person who did my job before me looked at cohorts for the past four years by looking at all the scores over four years, not respective of the transience of the number of children who came and left. Which is the most accurate when looking for trends? Any assistance would be appreciated.

With Ann Landers gone, who else is going to resolve arguments like this? I'm happy to say that you are right. A cohort comparison means "same child to same child" comparison. As you note, that involves a much smaller group of students than the universe of students with which you start unless you had a school with zero mobility. That cost in sample size reduction, however, is a price worth paying for greatly improved accuracy.

Look at it this way. If we were doing pharmaceutical research, and we wanted to study the impact of something (medicine, surgery, exercise, education, curriculum...) on a group of patients over four years, some of those patients might drop out of the study. But in order to have the most accurate analysis, we would stay with those students—I mean, patients—who started the study four years ago. We would not replace them with people who just happened to wander in later, but who had not had the four years of the treatment.

When it comes to reporting, you should address the concerns of those who allege that you are "ignoring" the mobile students by using the "two-column" technique, with column one for all students, and column two for only those students who have been continuously enrolled. While the trends may be similar, only the second column represents genuine impact of curriculum and teaching. By the way, the same is true of attendance corrections, with column one for all students and column two for only those students who attended school 90 percent or more (including students who show up half the time is the same error of including students who were not there for the curriculum and instruction you are purporting to measure).

81 We want to disaggregate student performance data for the past three years based on Free and Reduced Lunch status, as well as Limited English Proficiency and Special Education. Is it typical to compare each subgroup to the whole (i.e., all students) or to all students minus that subgroup? In other words, should I compare F&R students to all students, or to Paid Lunch students (which is essentially another subgroup)? If comparing them to all students, the F&R students are represented in both data sets. I ask primarily for graphing purposes, but my graphs will influence how the board and administration make data-driven decisions. Can you help?

I would suggest two comparisons. The first is the one you suggest: comparing the subgroup to the average of all students (that means all, including the subgroup). The second comparison is a listing of subgroups so that each group is mutually exclusive. That is typically the report that you will be required to file for the state and the No Child Left Behind Act.

82 **Regarding district-wide or school-wide summary growth data, what represents a statistically significant gain? For example, at School A, 77 percent of 3rd graders were proficient in reading in the fall, while 83 percent were proficient come spring. In School B, the fall figure was 88 percent proficient and spring was 90 percent proficient. Did either or both schools make statistically significant gains? Is there a formula or rule of thumb? Does it depend on "n" count?**

In the past we have been happy to report "gains at all schools/all grades/all subjects." Now we want to better characterize those gains. Any ideas?

The "rule of thumb" on statistical significance is a T-test that asks this question: "Is the difference from the first period to the second period 95 percent or more likely NOT due to random variation?" That is a statistical question that can vary with the sample size and the variation among the items in the sample. For example, the growth from 88 percent to 90 percent could be significant (that is, non-random) with 300 students and low variation, and it could be insignificant (that is, subject to random variation) with 30 students and high variation. So, unfortunately, there is no rule of thumb without doing the actual test.

There is a deeper question, however, and that is the use of MULTIPLE MEASURES to determine true growth. A single test, whether it is reading comprehension scores or blood pressure scores, does not give you the full picture. It is essential that you collect multiple measurements, including external data, internal data, and classroom data, and then triangulate all of these data points before you come to a conclusion. Even if a result of one test is "significant" in the statistical sense, it is nevertheless important to view multiple data sources before deciding whether true growth has been achieved.

83 **I need to test a hypothesis. I believe that more time spent with a particular curriculum program has resulted in higher vocabulary scores, but I would like to be able to back it up with proof. My question is, what do I ask teachers?**

1. **How much time each week have you spent on the program?**
2. **How many words do you currently have on your word wall?**
3. **How do you transfer the word wall into instruction?**
4. **How many days a week do you actually do the program?**
5. **In looking at your lesson plans, how many total days did you work with words?**

Should I ask all of these questions? If my hypothesis is correct, I should see higher vocabulary scores in those classes that actually implemented the program block at a higher level. Any feedback or suggestions would be greatly appreciated. I am looking forward to see if I can substantiate my FEELING about this!

I think you have much more than a "feeling" about the impact of your instructional practices on improved vocabulary scores. You have both external research and your own internal data to support your hypothesis.

The external research comes from Robert Marzano's new book, *What Works in Schools: Translating Research into Action*, and he specifically addresses the impact of instruction on vocabulary. Briefly, he says that context is not enough. Students need direct instruction and it makes a huge difference for them.

Your own internal research appears strong as well, but I understand your desire to document it better, so here are my suggestions:

Of all the things you list below, one that is easy and consistent is

TIME on the program. The others, particularly lesson plans, may be interesting for you to look at, but it's just not precise enough. The other thing that you don't have but I think is essential is a measurement of the degree of implementation of the program. In other words, you could have two teachers both of whom reported devoting twenty minutes to it, but who had dramatically different degrees of implementation. How do you specify degree of implementation? I think the best way is with a rubric that teachers themselves could develop. Just as we do for classroom assessment, use "Exemplary, Proficient, Progressing, and Not Meeting Standards" as the headings. Then work from the inside out. Start with "Proficient" and list all the characteristics of effective implementation. Use language that is clear, free of jargon, and that your newest student teacher could understand. Then describe "Progressing." It's pretty close, but just not as effective as we'd like to be. Then describe "Exemplary"—what the program looks like when you are really cooking—WAY beyond being proficient. Then describe "Not Meeting"—students are disengaged, just looking at the book, not learning, etc.

Now you'll have two measurements: time and effectiveness. In the end, we want to strive for both. Time without effectiveness isn't any good. And having great intentions for the vocabulary program without sufficient time doesn't help either.

This will not only give you solid research for your school accountability plan, but the exercise of describing effective teaching in vivid terms will help you and the teachers clarify expectations that you have of them and that they have of themselves.

Successful Schools: 90/90/90 and Beyond

Revisiting the 90/90/90 Schools

84 **In my district, the 90/90/90 studies are currently resurfacing as a topic of interest. Is there additional research since your original study?**

This year the International Reading Association is publishing a brief update of the original study. You can download a draft at www.MakingStandardsWork.com, click on "resources" and then see "High Performance in High Poverty Schools" and click the "new" button. It's a free download.

Please also see www.edtrust.org and the monograph, "Dispelling the Myth, Revisited."

An excellent source of updated information on success in high poverty schools is provided by the *Marshall Memo*, a weekly summary of relevant educational research. The editor, Kim Marshall, is very generous in providing free copies for inspection by prospective subscribers. You can e-mail him at kim.marshall8@verizon.net.

My new book, *Accountability for Learning* (ASCD, 2004), has some new research on this topic.

Of course, I would never suggest any single source of research, including my own, as the final word on this matter. The best that we can do is look at the preponderance of the evidence which appears to say the following:

1. Poverty and a home environment that lacks English language literacy have significantly adverse impacts on student achievement.

2. The impacts of poverty and the lack of an English language environment are not necessarily permanent and irreversible, but significant interventions are required. Short-term pullout programs, after school technology-based programs, and the like are not sufficient for the 12-year-old reading, if at all, on a

2nd grade reading level. Where there are significant gains in high-poverty, high-minority schools, there are intensive, long-term, and required intervention programs. Moreover, these interventions are part of the regular classroom day for every student, not just for a few who are identified as being "at risk."

3. Necessary interventions are misdirected or never started unless school leaders have consistent (monthly or quarterly) information on student achievement relative to state standards. Annual assessments are not enough.

I hope that this is of help. My work is a small pebble on a mountain of evidence on the subject. I would refer people to the work of Ron Edmonds that started three decades ago. My contribution has been very small indeed compared to that body of work.

85 **I would like to know where I can find a list of California 90/90/90 schools. I have seen it referenced in various articles, but I have not been able to find the list itself. Also, what were the criteria for meeting the 90 percent achievement?**

The best way to find schools that meet your criteria is in the "Dispelling the Myth" section of the interactive web site, www.edtrust.org.

HOWEVER, I want to be clear that the original 90/90/90 designation—90 percent free and reduced lunch, 90 percent minority enrollment, and 90 percent meeting or exceeding state standards—is not a "list" that we maintain. Schools throughout the nation meet this, and a few are kind enough to let me know about their success. An example in California is Mead Valley Elementary School, and the principal, Earl Shore, will be happy to speak with you. But there are many, many more success stories than this, and they simply remain anonymous. I was in New York City today, for example, and heard from a California administrator about their success in a high poverty, high minority school simply by the accident of running into him 3,000 miles away from his home.

The bottom line is this: There are thirty years of research studies of student success in high poverty, high minority schools. One more school or one more state or one more study doesn't really change the fundamental picture that emerges, and that is that teaching, curriculum, and leadership make a profound difference in student achievement, and those variables are more important than demographics. If the faculty believes the research, then another study is not necessary. If the faculty doesn't believe the research, then 1,000 more studies are not persuasive. I have seen faculties that are persuaded by evidence from other states, and I have seen faculties that are not persuaded by evidence from ten miles away with schools in the same district, same culture, same union agreements, same financial limitations, and same leadership. In other words, the location of the research is really not the issue.

86 **I am teaching developmentally disabled children and I feel that I am being given inappropriate directives and unreasonable expectations from my administrators, all in the name of higher expectations and the 90/90/90 research. So, have you thrown out the bell curve and decided that all children have exactly the same intelligence and that therefore intelligence does not matter? If that is the case, then are my children who have IQs of between 55 and 69 expected to learn in regular class as if they really have IQs of 100 as does every other child? Could you advise me as to what you tell teachers of developmentally disabled children? I need to talk to my administrators.**

Too many people take the "all children can learn" ideal and therefore presume that neurological challenges are irrelevant and that special education is nothing more than an institutionalized excuse. That has never been my position. At the same time, I have seen great special educators help students achieve far more than many other people had ever expected. So how do we resolve the tension between meeting the individual needs of children and the need for all children to have an opportunity for success? Here are some observations you might wish to consider:

1. Much of what is called "special education" I would call "good education." For example, special educators might look at an assignment that I created and say, "Doug, that's not one task, but is really four tasks for my students. If you would break it down into logical steps, you might give special education students a better chance at success." They are right. Of course, their logic applies not only to special education students, but to all students.

2. Time is a critically important adaptation. The standards never say, "students will write quickly" or "students will perform mathematical functions within five minutes." Standards require proficiency, not speed. I have witnessed students with learning disabilities and special needs achieve state standards when great educators are willing to give them not just an extra fifteen minutes, but multiple opportunities for success. What does "multiple" really mean in practice? It is not "infinite" opportunities, but it sometimes can be as many as six or nine iterations of the same task. It is never, ever a one shot assessment.

3. Learning disabilities are differential, just as exceptional student abilities are differential. As you know better than I do, the diagnosis of "learning disabled and gifted" is not unusual. This is consistent with the Gardner/Perkins research at Project Zero at Harvard (on the web at www.pz.harvard.edu) that indicates that the relationship among different intelligences is about zero. Students are strong in some areas and weak in others. Similarly, I hesitate to count a student as deficient in ALL areas when the diagnostic instrument probably addressed only a few areas of intelligence.

4. We must clearly distinguish between what you have described as "low IQ" and skill deficiency. I certainly agree that cognitive impairments are a reality. Students with fetal alcohol syndrome, crack addiction at birth, and other profound disabilities are a reality, and I have never pretended otherwise. At the same time, however, I am gravely concerned about the number of students whom I have seen labeled as "low IQ" who are, in fact, able to produce fine work, exceptional essays, creative art, and marvelous

musical, athletic, or technological performances, if only we give them the time to do so. You know your students better than I do, so I am not attempting to make an inappropriate generalization. I would only ask this question: Is there ANY area where these students are successful? Music? Nintendo? Peer relationships? Art? My challenge as a teacher is discovering their strengths and applying those strengths to their challenges.

5. Adaptations and accommodations are year-round requirements, not merely procedures for test week. In an astonishingly large number of schools, I have found that low performance by students with IEPs and 504s is associated with the fact that the adaptations and accommodations they used ONLY applied during test week. That is as unfair as expecting the football coach to conduct practices without a football, and then expressing shock and outrage when the players seemed confused on game day.

In sum, what do I say to teachers of developmentally disabled children? The first thing I say is "thank you." Next I assure them that I'm not trying to be oblivious to student needs. If they need more time and appropriate adaptations or accommodations, we must provide them. Most importantly, I need their expertise to help me define what a student CAN do. If the student cannot meet a standard, then break it down into ten increments and let me know what the student CAN achieve, what the student can partially achieve, and what the student has not yet achieved.

87 **I am interested in sources about urban high schools with over 2000 students, ethnically diverse, and high-poverty populations that are successfully reaching high standards. Can you help me?**

For the latest information on this subject, see the web site www.edtrust.org, and select "Dispelling the Myth, Revisited." Where I see great things happening in equity and opportunity at the secondary level, there are these common characteristics:

1. More time: Kids can do algebra, biology, and for that matter, freshman English, but some of us need more time. We can do that in one of two ways: by providing time AFTER the student flunks the class, or BEFORE the failure. I favor the latter approach. This is the essence of "de-tracking": getting kids off the failure track and into an opportunity for success. With more time, we can cut the number of course failures by half.

2. Literacy intervention: If an 8th grader is not a proficient reader, there is an 85 percent probability that the student will remain non-proficient throughout high school (*Journal of Educational Psychology*, December 2001). Therefore, the most successful programs provide intensive, mandatory intervention. This might include double or triple literacy classes and self-contained classes if necessary.

3. Deferred science and social studies. If a student cannot read high school material, the failure will not only occur in 9th grade English, but also in other reading-intensive subjects. Defer 9th grade science and social studies to 10th grade, and replace these subjects with intensive literacy intervention. This is not because we disrespect science and social studies, but because those disciplines are so important that students should be able to read the textbooks before they take the classes.

88 **Can you refer me to any 90/90/90 middle schools or high schools? Most of what I have read about 90/90/90 schools is in reference to elementary schools. We have three high schools in our district with high poverty, high minority numbers, and we are hoping to visit similar high schools experiencing high academic achievement.**

There are, in fact, successful high poverty middle schools around the country. One updated source of that information is at www.edtrust.org. They have an interactive web site called, "Dispelling the Myth, Revisited." But California has recently released new Academic Performance Index results and there are several middle and high schools with significant performance improvements based on the issues we have long discussed: more time, focused curriculum, extra literacy and math, and nonfiction writing (with editing and rewriting) in every single class.

I do want to share my concern with visiting other schools. There were literally busloads of people who have been to Milwaukee (and Pueblo, Santa Ana, Riverview, Texas, Norfolk, Indianapolis, and many other places where we have documented success). The people who believed said, "Sure, we can do that. They are no smarter than we are. We could have spent the money internally!" The disbelievers say, "Sure, they are doing well, but we're different, and their success doesn't tell us anything." The second group is never convinced by visits any more than they are by my evidence from multiple schools. That's why leaders need to focus on behavior, not attitudes. The behavior comes first, then local success and then—only then—will the cynics get on board. And some of them will never be on board. What's stunning to me is that even when some cynics actually see improvement (they groaned and moaned and still got good results) they are still mad and won't give themselves and their professional practices credit: "They must have made the test easier," or "This year's crop of kids is better." It goes on and on.

So, back to your original request. The current superintendent of Milwaukee is Bill Andrikopolous. He was the former principal at a high poverty middle school in Milwaukee. He is a brilliant and generous guy who would give you some great ideas. But I don't want you to hold out hope that visits are the answer.

89 As a new school (this is our inaugural year) whose students already have high test scores, I believe we have a real opportunity to lay a strong foundation with our school improvement plan and the process of making that plan. Can you give me some advice or suggest books or research we might use to guide our process? I would like to base the creation of our team and the subsequent school improvement plan on a proven system.

In researching through my own library, I have spent some time with Marzano's *What Works in Schools*. Would you suggest this work for a book study by the school improvement team? Do you have other suggestions?

I strongly agree with your use of Bob Marzano's terrific book. In addition, you might want to review Mike Schmoker's *Results Fieldbook* and a couple of my recent books, *The Leader's Guide to Standards* and *The Daily Disciplines of Leadership*.

With regard to your specific questions:

1. For the planning process, keep it simple with a clear mission and vision that people understand, and a few measurable objectives that you can examine every month. It's better to have five or six objectives (such as the percentage of students proficient or higher in nonfiction writing or even the percentage of students who are advanced) that you measure every month than a huge laundry list of objectives that you examine once a year.

2. Balance academic, behavior, parent involvement, and teaching strategy issues. You are measuring much, much more than state test scores. This will allow you to have meaningful indicators at all levels.

3. Keep the focus on meeting rigorous standards at the proficient and advanced level, not on the other schools that

you beat. In the context you describe, your greatest challenge is complacency because students walk in the door with the proclivity for high test scores. By using standards, particularly with rigorous application and clear definition of "exemplary" or "advanced" or other words that challenge students and teachers to be more than "proficient," you can improve achievement and demonstrate that you are adding value to each student.

 90 **Our public junior high is contemplating going to an 'academy' style school. Where can I find good sources of 'schools that work' and 'best practices?' Our teachers will be able to design our own plan and we need help dreaming of the possible and thinking outside the box. What awesome ideas are going on out there that we could implement?**

Based on my direct observations in schools, let me offer the following considerations:

1. Academies define scenarios, not curriculum. Students will be responsible for core academic content standards in English, math, science, and social studies, though the context may change from law to technology to medicine to fine arts. For more detail on the development of engaging scenarios, please see *Making Standards Work*.

2. Academies help students and parents exercise choice, something that we know is strongly related to adolescent motivation and engagement. That only works, of course, if you are willing to arrange the school so that a very high percentage (90 percent or more) of students get their first choice. This means accepting that fact that not every academy will be of equal size or popularity, and that some academies may, in the course of time, be replaced by others.

3. An "academy fair" in the spring is a great way to introduce these ideas so that students can become exposed to

different contexts in which core academic content is taught. Make it exciting, modeled on registration for college classes. Choice, opportunity, personal independence: these are things that students love.

4. Give teachers TIME to develop new curriculum, scenarios, and assessments. This is an extraordinarily challenging leap from "do the Pythagorean Theorem because it might be on the test" to "Today we're working on an engineering problem for the new airport we are designing" (and, by the way, that includes learning and applying the Pythagorean Theorem).

In addition, you might want to consider www.nassp.org and www.ascd.org as excellent resources for examples of secondary school academies. In particular, you can search past issues of NASSP *Bulletin* and *Educational Leadership*. Hope this helps.

91 What private schools in New England are considered to be the very best in regard to standards and student achievement? What practices do they have in place to ensure the students become proficient in the standards? I would like the names of the schools, as we would like to contact each of them regarding their standards and practices.

The only better way to start a fight around here than to choose one prep school over another is to root for the Yankees or Cubs. Nevertheless, let me offer some ideas for you to consider.

First, we should cast a wider net than New England for the most successful schools. If you are looking for the top tier internationally, I would include not only the usual suspects in New England (Phillips, Tower, Andover, Exeter, Wheeler, Pingree) but also Harvard-Westlake in Los Angeles, Colorado Academy in Denver, Sidwell Friends in Washington, DC, Hong Kong International School, and Cairo American College (which is a K-12 international school). This list would undoubtedly get me into deep trouble with many other successful private schools, but it is just a start. What is interesting, however, is the number of public schools that have emulated the successful practices of private schools. For example, Roxbury Academy is a public school in Boston that has the highest African-American achievement in the state and a very high number of students eligible for free or reduced lunch.

I have not done a systematic research study on these schools, but even the most casual observer will note some things in common:

1. Writing: If you're familiar with my research, you know that I have linked writing and particularly nonfiction writing to student success in a variety of other areas. The quantity and quality of writing in the schools I have noted above is exceptional. For some excellent examples, please see a recent issue of the *Concord Review*, a publication of the nation's finest secondary school writing. Almost every issue will contain essays by the students in these schools and a number of public schools.

2. Well-rounded students: Contrary to myth, these schools are not SAT factories for the Ivy League. At most of them, physical education is required, as is involvement in art, drama, music, and other extracurricular activities. Students routinely take one or more world languages, are involved in multiple extracurricular activities, and know that school is about much more than test scores.

3. Relentless pursuit of standards: When students are not proficient in the most successful schools, they don't return home with a bad report card and a note saying that the $40,000 tuition check has been cashed. They receive intensive intervention and support in small groups, large groups, and as individuals.

4. Pre-assessment: We briefly considered sending our daughter to one of the schools noted above. Although she decided to remain in public school, I was very impressed by the pre-assessment process that included not only the typical math and verbal tests, but extensive interviews, art, writing, and interest inventories. The school invested a great deal of time BEFORE THE FIRST DAY OF SCHOOL to get to know the needs and interests of their students.

Note that I did not include that the parents are all rich and deeply involved. They aren't. There are kids who grew up in million dollar homes whose parents are utterly disengaged from school life, and parent involvement is a challenge at any level. All of these schools also have scholarship programs and, most importantly, none of the professional practices I noted above is unique to the private school setting.

Let me again emphasize that I do not work extensively with private schools and do not claim expertise in them. These are my general observations, not inferences based on systematic research. For additional information, I might recommend that you consider the web sites and catalogs of these schools and note the commonalties among them.

92 **Could you please email to us your definition of 'academic'? We are hoping to clear up the concerns that have arisen and are threatening to impede the progress and acceptance of standards-based education here at our school.**

I've written and spoken extensively about the importance of music, art, PE, world languages, technology, and other subjects. The bottom line is this: There is no such thing as a "nonacademic" subject in school. In fact, the evidence is clear that in the most successful schools that we have studied, music, art, and PE, among other subjects, are key to improving student success. The most successful practices we have seen are those in which faculty members explicitly embrace academic standards. Examples include:

- In art class, having students complete written assignments in which they compare and contrast different media and different artists.

- In music, having students explicitly recognize the relationship of note values to fractions to clapping rhythms.

- In PE, having students understand the relationships of metric and English measurements.

These are just a few examples among many—I never intend to marginalize or minimize the importance of the arts or other subjects. But I insist that they are all part of the development of the intellectual and emotional progress of each child. In the nation's leading schools, the faculty is not divided among those who are "academic" and those who are not, but rather all faculty members devote themselves to the success of individual student development. That's the way it should be in every public school.

 93 **In your opinion, what should be the elements of a middle school schedule that best support standards, assessment, and achievement?**

 Here's a start:

1. Flexibility: We should not assume that every middle school student learns at the same rate or that they enter middle school with the same background. If I have a 7th grader on a 4th grade reading level, then it's clear that the student needs more than one period per day of language arts. "Reading across the curriculum" is not enough; this student needs more time to develop reading skills. We must stop the one-size-fits-all school of scheduling.

2. Sense of purpose: We must be clear about the fundamental purpose of middle school. It is not, as one middle school principal told me, "to build self-esteem," at least not directly. Rather, the fundamental purpose of middle school is to have students enter high school with confidence and success. If we (I speak as a former middle school math teacher) do that well, then we will also build their self-esteem. If we fail to send them to high school with confidence and success, then all of our psychological efforts will be for naught.

3. Prioritization: We must be frank. Not every subject is of equal value. Literacy is primary and math is a close second. I know of many middle schools that are taking traditional electives such as family and consumer sciences, metal

shop, and wood shop, and transferring them to high school—and late in high school at that—11th and 12th grade. The students who are in those classes need to be able to READ. It is simply offensive that students who are 11 and 12 years of age are being identified as "low potential" and being tracked into low expectation classes under the guise of sympathy and sensitivity. I ask this essential question: If this were a private middle school for rich kids, what would your curriculum be? Do your students in your public school deserve anything different?

94 **Would you ever suggest blocks of time for grades K-8 for content areas, especially math and literacy? We are thinking of introducing a ninety-minute-per-day math/ literacy block for elementary grades.**

Thanks very much for your inquiry. There is no question that time—significant blocks of time focused on skill building, grouping, and regrouping—influences student achievement. In my new book, *Accountability for Learning*, I elaborate on this theme. Briefly, the research suggests the following:

At the elementary level, three hours per day of "prime time" learning, typically 8:30-11:30 a.m., should be devoted to literacy, with two hours on reading and one hour on writing. At the secondary level, students should receive double classes in literacy. This might be both the traditional English Literature class and also a class in writing, reading, or other appropriate literacy-centered subjects. If students have a literacy deficit in secondary school, they spent more than a decade getting into that problem and they are unlikely to get out of it in summer school. We have seen similarly successful results when schools have doubled the amount of time they devote to math. Failure rates are dramatically reduced if we give students more time.

The objections to this emphasis on literacy and math is typically that "we won't be able to cover all the science and social studies standards" and "we won't have time for electives." My responses are as follows:

1. Students who can't read the textbook are unlikely to be successful in science and social studies. Literacy comes first. No high school science or social studies teacher has ever lamented the inability of incoming students to recall Boyle's Law, but plenty of these teachers have deeply regretted the inability of students to read and write.

2. Students who drop out of school don't take electives. I'm not advocating the elimination of elective courses, but I do strongly suggest that we need fewer electives in grades 9 and 10, and thereby can have more opportunities for electives in grades 11 and 12.

3. Music, art, PE, technology, world languages, and other courses remain essential, but they are there to SUPPORT fundamental standards in literacy and math, not to supplant those courses. In the end, we are not teachers of a subject such as math, music, or PE; rather, we are teachers of students, and must use our skills to meet the needs of those students.

Show Me the Proof!

95   **As assistant superintendent in an elementary district, I am quite interested in using some of the strategies related to "90/90/90 schools," high-poverty and minority schools that are also high-achieving. However, I have found no specific descriptions of the programs in those schools and no references to the original research. Can you provide citations or refer me to the schools that participated in the studies?**

The first 90/90/90 research was in the book, *Accountability in Action: A Blueprint for Learning Organizations.* The chapter on the 90/90/90 schools is available as a free download at www.MakingStandardsWork.com.

HOWEVER, and this is a big however, I would never encourage any school leader to rely on a single source for strategies in high poverty schools. My studies are just a pebble on a mountain of evidence on this subject that goes back three decades. My research has also been replicated by many schools throughout the country with remarkably similar results. Most recently, urban districts such as Norfolk, Santa Ana, Indianapolis, and St. Louis have all reported similar findings in those schools that were willing to make dramatic changes in their emphasis on student achievement, nonfiction writing, collaborative scoring, and multiple opportunities for success. We regularly document these in our free newsletter, *Focus on Achievement*, that goes out to 20,000 educators and school leaders each quarter, and we would be happy to send you copies as well. In addition to my work, please see www.edtrust.org for the reports "Dispelling the Myth" and "Dispelling the Myth, Revisited." Finally, you might want to consider two books from Jossey-Bass: *The Daily Disciplines of Leadership* and *The Leader's Guide to Standards*.

Uniting Stakeholders for Student Achievement

The National Level

96 **What is your perspective on George Bush's No Child Left Behind Act and how it relates to Title I?**

You can start by taking a look at my book, *Crusade in the Classroom: How George W. Bush's Education Reforms Will Affect Your Children, Our Schools*.

With regard to the Title I and other federal issues, I only attempt to remind people that this is no more the "Bush Bill" that it is the Kennedy, Lieberman, or Clinton bill. I know that many educators prefer just to be angry with Bush for the testing, but such a position neglects the fact that 90 percent of Democrats in the House and Senate voted for this thing as well. In addition, the signature on the executive order that is in the news (the one that permits parents to change schools after their children are in a Title 1 school without Adequate Yearly Progress for two years) belongs to Bill Clinton, not George W. Bush. So, we can't be mad at him for implementing educational policy that is manifestly the same as his predecessor's.

97 **How are you able to derive a national standard from a state test?**

With regard to the issue of state vs. national standards, the only standards in use in testing are state standards. Despite numerous assertions to the contrary, there are no "national standards" in federal law or elsewhere. Federal legislation requires that state assessments are based on state standards. There are a number of model standards at the national level, but they are no more than "national suggestions," not national standards.

98 Here in California, there is a theme of conversation associated with the levels of challenge and expectations in the state's curriculum content standards. Has anyone done an analysis to align the comparable rigor of standards across the states? If California's standards are "more rigorous," then we have some reason to understand why in some states in the nation there is a report that no students are "below proficient." Can you help direct me to this kind of answer/information?

The most comprehensive analysis comparing state standards was done by Achieve, Inc. and was published in the "Quality Counts" issue of *Education Week*. You can download it at www.edweek.org. You can also find similar information at www.edexcellence.net. California was one of three states to receive an "A" rating for its standards.

HOWEVER, some notes of caution are in order. First, it is easy to conflate rigor and quantity. The three states that have high rates also happen to have voluminous standards which are not necessarily related to the amount of time available in the school year. For a detailed analysis of this problem, see Robert Marzano's recent writings, including book *What Works in Schools* published by ASCD.

Second, it is easy to conflate rigor and specificity. California does earn high ratings for the clarity and specificity of its standards. But that does not necessarily make them more rigorous than Wisconsin's, which are more general.

Third, the estimates of proficiency by states are not reflections of rigor at all. As you note, some states say that every school is performing at an acceptable level, while other states have consigned the majority of their schools to "underperforming" status. The truth is that when ANY exam is administered the first time, scores tend to be low, because teaching has not been adequately aligned with that assessment. Over the course of time, however, instruction, classroom assessment, and state assessment tend to become aligned better and scores go up. Thus the differences you see among states tend to reflect how long they have had the same exam, not necessarily the relative rigor of those examinations.

Fourth and most importantly, standards alone have "rigor" only in the sense that a city health code has "rigor": It's a great idea in theory, but it does you little good if you're the guy with food poisoning. To extend the analogy, no matter what the health regulations say, they are only as good as the implementation in the individual restaurant. There can be a lot of creativity in menu, presentation, and atmosphere, but you don't want a whole lot of creativity in hygiene. There, you want consistency. When standards are done well, there is also plenty of room for creativity in teaching strategies, scenario building, and practices to improve student engagement. But there is absolute consistency in core expectations, such as reading levels and writing proficiency. There is always tension between these two competing demands of consistency and creativity, and thus people in positions of leadership such as yourself must perfect the art of making everyone equally mad at you!

Fifth and finally, no one would argue that the California standards, however highly rated, are perfect. However, my response to the critics is that before we reject standards entirely, we must consider the alternative. As flawed as some state standards may be, at least they express a consistent expectation for student performance. Without them, we are left with idiosyncratic expectations and the comparison of students to one another on the bell curve. Although the present state of standards is far from ideal, it is superior to the bell curve and expectations of students which vary from one classroom and neighborhood to the next.

Teachers and Other Personnel

99 I am non-instructional personnel, in the Information Technology Department, and feel like I have little input. The information discussed by the majority of educators is not filtered down to us, so we end up making decisions that do not concur with the faculty, nor they with ours. I was wondering what methods or practices you can suggest that would bridge that gap. Perhaps it is a common problem that has no solutions, but I feel I could provide valuable information and tactics if given the opportunity. What are your thoughts?

The phenomenon you have described, a disconnection between technology (and the way we implement it and measure it) and classroom teachers, is a national problem. In fact, I wrote a case study about it in my book, *Accountability in Action* (Chapter 17). The issues you have addressed must be addressed with faculty and administrators. Part of the problem is an historical one: Technology went from being a scary anomaly in schools to being the domain of the business department to being part of a central office instructional technology domain to finally being part of the daily classroom reality. But the transition among those four phases has left a lot of problems, including bureaucratic tangles and poor communication, in its wake. Let's rethink what technology really is: the #2 pencil of the 21st century.

One hundred years ago, nobody measured educational progress by counting the number of #2 pencils or referring all inquiries to the "Department of #2 Pencils," but we rather quickly integrated that "new" technology into the classroom. I would suggest that we rethink the way that we manage instructional technology, and EXPLICITLY include people such as yourself and other technology experts as part of school-based instructional teams. That means sharing staff development, faculty meetings, and other daily activities of teachers. The library/media center is the ideal hub of technology activity, integrating literacy, research, assessment, and other classroom-level activities with the Internet and other technological resources. It also means inviting you to the same staff development—not just in technology, but in content areas and in teaching strategies—that we have for classroom educators.

We're a team, and we all have the same focus: improving student achievement. Only a clear changing of traditional organizational boundaries will allow that team to flourish.

100 **I would like to try a school-wide focus for professional development this year rather than have each teacher write an individual professional goal. Does this sound reasonable? What focus areas would have the greatest impact? Our test scores overall have been below the district for last spring. I would like a school-wide focus on reading and assessment.**

You can have both a school-wide focus on professional development and at the same time recognize the individual needs of your teachers. It is similar to what we do in the classroom when we have the same academic standards for all students, but take steps to differentiate instruction where it is appropriate.

The place to start is with a teacher self-assessment. Identify your most important areas for professional development focus. I would nominate the following:

1. Classroom assessment techniques, with an emphasis on the creation of standards-based assessments for classroom use and immediate student feedback.

2. Collaborative scoring of student work, with an emphasis on the development of common scoring guides that can be used by several teachers (and parents and students!) to evaluate student work consistently.

3. Improved student writing, with an emphasis on writing in every (and I mean every) curriculum area using a common scoring guide and consistent scoring.

You may add some others, such as classroom management, parent communication, math problem-solving, or familiarization with the state test. The key is that you do not open the door to just ANYTHING, but create a framework within which professional development will take place this year. Within that framework, teachers have choice. Outside of that framework, they should not ask you for time and resources to support it.

Once your have identified these areas, let each teacher conduct a self-assessment, rating themselves 1 - 4 as follows:

- 4—I routinely do this in the classroom and am confident in my skills. In fact, I'm willing to lead our building-based staff development in this area and would be happy to teach some of the professional development sessions on this.

- 3—I use this in the classroom, but I am not confident enough to teach this to my colleagues yet.

- 2—I have had some training on this subject, but I don't use it in the classroom very much.

- 1—I am not familiar with this and need some fundamental training.

Once you have done this, you have both a school-wide focus on the things that are most important and you have also taken into consideration the individual needs of teachers. Of course, teachers can still seek professional development independently, but their requests should be within the framework of the most important areas you have established.

 101 **Our district is asking our teachers to follow a 'pacing plan' by which all of the teachers must teach the same lessons the same day the entire school year. There is very little wiggle room in this plan. What are your thoughts on this?**

There is room for compromise. I agree that we need to agree, perhaps once a month or once a quarter, about where we should be. That assures equity for all students, regardless of teacher or neighborhood. But on a day-to-day basis, I need the freedom to stop, recognize a mistake, re-teach, rearrange my schedule, ask my colleagues for help, and meet my students' needs.

Let me give you an example that happened to me frequently. You'd think I would have figured it out after all these years, but it happened ALL THE TIME. I would plan a unit for 6th grade students on exponents—a critically important concept to get them ready for algebra in 8th or 9th grade. I'd find that half of them had poor multiplication skills, and you can't do exponents or test the reasonability of answers without knowing multiplication. Sometimes I'd have to spend four weeks on a lesson I thought would take one or two weeks. That sort of thing happens to teachers all the time, and if I just said "Sorry, you missed it, we're moving on," then half my class would have been discouraged, demoralized, and worst of all, not been proficient in math. So I had to have the freedom to figure out how to take extra time in math, how to ask friends in music and PE to help me out, how to integrate math problems into social studies and science. I'm not saying it was perfect, but there is a lot to be said for admitting a problem (my students were not where I thought they were) and figuring out a solution (take extra time, collaborate with colleagues) rather than just charging ahead with the schedule.

102 I am the principal at a high school where my staff is difficult to change. Sometimes they think they know it all. However, last month, we reviewed our school data and talked in groups about what the word 'proficient' means to them. We will then discuss student work (shuffled, with names removed) and try to agree on a definition of proficiency so that we can all tell whether our students are meeting standards.

What am I missing here? How can I be more structured so when the teachers look at the student samples they know exactly what to look for and what to do?

First, congratulations on your terrific initiative! You clearly have the right components in place. You are looking at student work and you are committed to collaboration. Moreover, you have created a safe way for teachers to share student work because you are making the submissions anonymous so that neither the identity of the student nor the teacher is disclosed.

You asked for some ways of adding structure to this process, so let me share what I do in these circumstances.

First, I hand out a single piece of student work—remember that all of the samples should have started life as "proficient"—and ask each teacher to evaluate it ALONE, using the scoring rubric that was used for the assessment. I then track the percentage of faculty members who rated that piece of work Exemplary, Proficient, Progressing, or Not Meeting Standards. I note the percentage of agreement, which is typically fairly low.

Second, I give teachers the opportunity to score the assessment collaboratively in groups of two or three, and make any revisions they wish. I note the percentage of agreement again. At this point it is typically a little bit better.

Third, we have a group meeting to revise the scoring rubric. The theme of this meeting is "the enemy is not each other; the enemy is ambiguity." Where there is a disagreement it is not the fault of the teacher, but the fault of an ambiguous scoring rubric. We use a collaborative process to revise and improve the scoring rubric, making it more specific. Then we score the same piece of work AGAIN. The third time, the level of agreement is always higher than the first two times.

Finally, we look at this process from the student's point of view. What would they think of the first level of scoring? Pretty unfair, right? As we worked together, collaborated, and refined the rubric, our fairness improved. This process is not about some state mandate, but about our fundamental, shared value of FAIRNESS.

In most schools, this takes ALL YEAR LONG—it's not one, short staff development meeting. Some districts open EVERY faculty meeting, including cabinet meetings at the central office, with collaborative scoring of student work. They learn that the faster they reach 80 percent consensus, the faster they move on to other agenda items.

103 **I am dealing with a group of high school teachers who are very angry about having to do some collaboratively-scored writing and reading assessments. They see it as 'teaching to the test' and have even gone so far as to write an open letter in the local papers claiming that the central office is taking all of the creativity out of the classroom by doing this work. I will be meeting with this staff soon and would love to have some of your research at my fingertips. Could you please let me know where I can get my hands on the appropriate studies or other possible sources?**

There is an abundant body of research on the value of literacy and writing in particular. Frankly, it's just common sense that students who do more nonfiction writing, along with editing and rewriting, will improve thinking and reasoning skills, which will in turn improve their abilities in science, social studies, mathematics, and everything else that they do in life. But if people need to see published resources, I would recommend the following:

- Calkins, Lucy, *The Art of Teaching Writing* (Heinemann, 1996)

- Darling-Hammond, Linda, *The Right to Learn* (Jossey-Bass, 1997)

- Reeves, D., "Standards are not enough." (NASSP *Bulletin*, December 2000)

- Reeves, D. *The Leader's Guide to Standards*. (Jossey-Bass, 2002)

Here are some ideas to compromise with teachers on the issue of maintaining their creativity while simultaneously maintaining a commitment to excellence:

1. Allow teachers to choose the prompt so that the writing assignments fit into their subject. Everyone uses the same scoring rubric, of course, in order to maintain consistency of expectations. But the subject matter of the prompt can be selected by the teachers.

2. Allow teachers outside of language arts to use an abbreviated scoring rubric, focusing primarily on organization and conventions. Some of the complexities of the traditional rubrics can be overwhelming for people outside of language arts.

3. Allow team scoring so that the same assignment receives credit in both science and language arts, for example, and teachers score them together.

4. Give up time in faculty meetings for collaborative scoring so that teachers know that the administration is willing to give up its meeting so that teachers will have more time. The same can be done with perhaps half of the building and district professional development hours.

These are all reasonable compromises that show your good faith. The essential question that every teacher must address is this: Is what we have been doing in the past working? Are our students writing well enough to have opportunities beyond high school? Ask some local community college and university and technical school faculty to talk with you about this issue. They will uniformly report that even students with good work ethic and decent test scores are writing abysmally, and that this is hurting the career and academic opportunities for these students. The remedy for this is more writing, more editing, more feedback—and all of those things in more subjects. Do you have more 9th graders than 12th graders? In virtually every high school in the land, the answer is yes, and that is because students who do not succeed in 9th and 10th grades tend to drop out. These students are not stupid, but they lack essential skills for success in school and in life, and our failure to intervene to give them those skills results in a lifetime of adverse consequences for them.

One final note: The thesis of the "we can't be creative" argument is that because of the demands of standards, you just can't be creative but only must teach to the test all day. If that thesis were true, then the evidence should indicate that teachers who do mindless test drills all day long have higher test scores than teachers whose classrooms are marked by creativity, thinking, engagement, analysis, rigor, communication, and, of course, writing. After all, their reasoning goes, you just don't have time for all those good things if you are doing test drills, and the test drills are the only way to have high scores. In fact, the evidence is the opposite of that hypothesis. I'm advocating FOR creativity, and writing, thinking, engagement, and analysis are all parts of a creative classroom.

Parental Support

 104 **I am considering implementing a "family support scale" to be used in understanding some of the antecedents of test performance. Can I get some suggestions for this scale to use with the parents in my district?**

I've seen several different varieties of this. Ultimately you will want to tailor it to the needs of your district and have input from parents and teachers. Nevertheless, here are some ideas to consider:

1. In a "Parent Report Card," parents self-report responses to questions such as "I review my child's homework every night," "I prevent my child from having access to alcohol, tobacco, and drugs," and "I personally contact my child's teacher if I notice my child's school performance is slipping." These can have simple responses such as "Always, sometimes, or never."

2. In a "Parent Engagement Record," parents agree at the beginning of the school year to be actively engaged in school for a certain number of hours (a good standard is nine hours for the year—an average of just an hour a month and pretty easy for most people to do). The key is "actively engaged"— not simply attending an event, but participating with students. This might be listening to them read in a small group, participating in a secondary school panel to review a student's end-of-course project, participating in mock job interviews with students, or attending lunch in the school cafeteria and asking students to tell the adult about their plans beyond school. In addition, parent engagement can include adult education programs such as parent effectiveness, technology, or student assessment programs.

When schools set a standard for parent engagement, they must deliberately create programs that will have more parents (or significant adults) involved and then can relate the extent of that involvement to student academic performance. Although this involves some extra work up front, teachers report that their lives are much easier when parents are actively involved and when they proactively communicate about student academic issues.

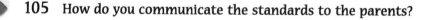

105 How do you communicate the standards to the parents?

The best example of this I've seen is the "Refrigerator Curriculum." Districts took the state standards for each grade and reduced them to a single page of "What your child needs to know and be able to do" for each grade. Of course, they do not list every single standard, but they list the most important ones that EVERY student should be mastering. It's also important to help parents understand why standards are so important: They are fair and effective. For more elaboration on communicating about standards with parents and other stakeholders, see the book *The Leader's Guide to Standards* published by Jossey-Bass.

References

Books and Articles

Ainsworth, L. (2003). *Power standards*. Denver, CO: Advanced Learning Press.

Ainsworth, L. (2003). *Unwrapping the standards*. Denver, CO: Advanced Learning Press.

Amaral, O. M., Garrison, L., & Klentschy, M. (2002, Summer). Helping English learners increase achievement through inquiry-based science instruction. *Bilingual Research Journal*, *26* (2), 213-239.

Anderson, R. C., Wilson, P., & Fielding, L. (1988). Growth in reading and how children spend their time outside of school. *Reading Research Quarterly*, *23*(3), 285-303.

Calkins, L. (1983). *Lessons from a child*. Portsmouth, NH: Heinemann.

Calkins, L. (1994). *The art of teaching writing*. Portsmouth, NH: Heinemann.

Calkins, L. (2000). *The art of teaching reading*. Upper Saddle River, NJ: Longman.

Capella, E., & Weinstein, R.S. (2001). Turning around reading achievement: Predictors of high school students' academic resilience. *Journal of Educational Psychology*, *93*(4), 758-771.

Darling-Hammond, L. (1997). *The right to learn*. San Fransisco: Jossey-Bass.

Edwards, V. B. (Ed.). (2004, January 8). Quality counts 2004: Count me in: Special education in an era of standards [special report]. *Education Week*, *23* (17).

Guay, F., Marsh, H. W., & Boivin, M. (2003, March). Academic self-concept and academic achievement: Developmental perspectives on their causal ordering. *Journal of Educational Psychology*, *95* (1).

Guskey, T. & Bailey, J. (2001). *Developing grading and reporting systems for student learning*. Thousand Oaks, CA: Corwin Press.

Hacsi, T. (2002). *Children as pawns: The policies of education reform*. Cambridge: Harvard University Press.

Hiebert, J., & Stigler, J. W. (1999). *The teaching gap: Best ideas from the world's teachers for improving education in the classroom*. New York: Free Press.

Hirsch E. D., (1996). *The schools we need: And why we don't have them*. New York: Doubleday.

Johnston, R. C. (2000, October 18). As studies stress link to scores, districts get tough on attendance. *Education Week*, *20* (7), 1, 10.

Kurdek, L. A., & Sinclair, R. J. (2001, September). Predicting reading and mathematic achievement in fourth-grade children from kindergarten readiness scores. *Journal of Educational Psychology*, *93* (3), 451-455.

Levine, M. (2003). *The myth of laziness*. New York: Simon and Schuster.

Linton Professional Development Corporation (Producer and Director). (1998). *Standards that work, Volume 802*. [Videotape].

Linton Professional Development Corporation (Producer and Director). (1998). *Standards that work, Volume 803*. [Videotape].

Manzo, K. K. (2002, November 20). Relegating student research to the past. *Education Week 12* (22), 1, 12.

Marzano, R. & Pickering, D. (2001). *Classroom instruction that works: Research-based strategies for increasing student achievement*. Alexandria, VA: ASCD.

Marzano, R. (2003). *What works in schools: Translating research into action*. Alexandria, VA: ASCD.

Marzano, R., Marzano, J, & Pickering, D. (2003). *Classroom management that works: Research-based strategies for every teacher*. Alexandria, VA: ASCD.

Reeves, D. B. (2000). *Accountability in action: A blueprint for learning organizations*. Denver, CO: Advanced Learning Press.

Reeves, D. B. (2000, December). Standards are not enough: Essential transformations for school success. *NASSP Bulletin, 84*, 5-19.

Reeves, D. B. (2001). *Crusade in the classroom: How George W. Bush's education policies will affect your child*. New York: Kaplan.

Reeves, D. B. (2002). *Making standards work: How to implement standards-based assessments in the classroom, school, and district*. (3rd ed.). Denver, CO: Advanced Learning Press.

Reeves, D.B. (2002). *Reason to write: Help your child succeed in school and in life through better reasoning and clear communication*. New York: Kaplan.

Reeves, D.B. (2002). *Reason to write: Student handbook*. New York: Kaplan.

Reeves, D. B. (2002). *The daily disciplines of leadership: How to improve student achievement, staff motivation, and personal organization*. San Francisco: Jossey-Bass.

Reeves, D. B. (2002). *The leader's guide to standards: A blueprint for educational equity and excellence*. San Francisco: Jossey-Bass.

Schmoker, M. J. (2001). *The results fieldbook: Practical strategies from dramatically improved schools*. Alexandria, VA: ASCD.

Slavin, R. (2002). *Educational psychology*. (7th ed.). Upper Saddle River, NJ: Allyn & Bacon.

Spandel, V. (2003). *Creating young writers*. Upper Saddle River, NJ: Allyn & Bacon.

Websites

Project Zero at the Harvard Graduate School of Education:
www.pz.harvard.edu

The Association for Supervision and Curriculum Development:
www.ascd.org

The Center for Performance Assessment:
www.makingstandardswork.com.

The Education Trust:
www.edtrust.org

Educational Resources Information Center (ERIC):
http://eric.ed.gov/

The National Association of Secondary School Principals:
www.nassp.org

The Thomas B. Fordham Foundation:
www.edexcellence.net

Trends in International Math and Science Study:
http://isc.bc.edu/timss2003.html

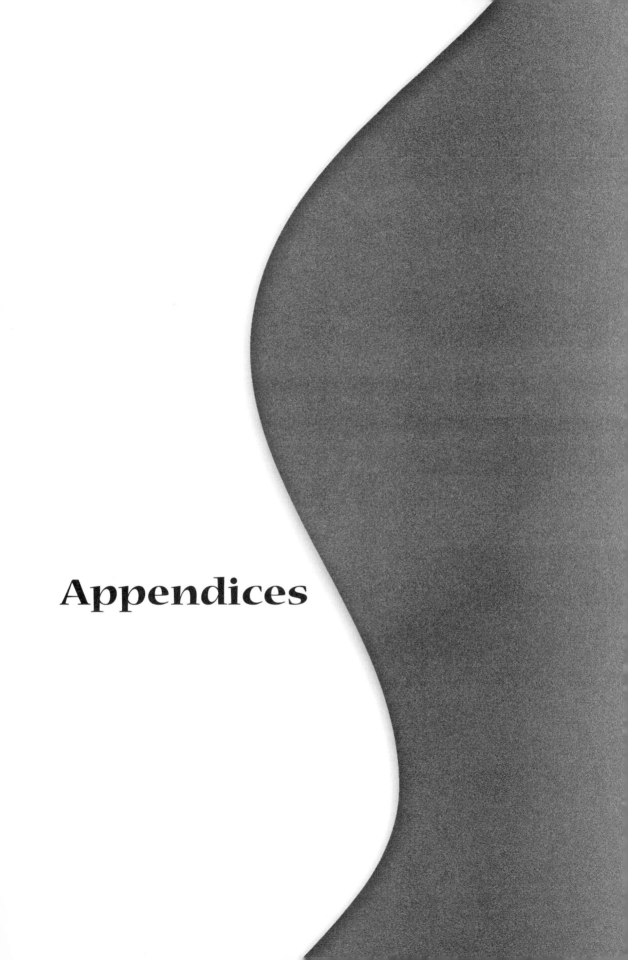

Appendices

Appendix A:
List of Questions by Chapter

Chapter 1: Power Standards

1. We have been working with the concept of Power Standards in our district, and the following questions have come up: What are the differences between Power Standards, essential learnings, common outcomes, viable curriculum, learning targets, etc.? Or are they different ways of stating and answering the question, "What are the core things we want all kids to learn as a result of instruction?"

2. Could you relate to me your basic philosophy behind the credibility of standards if they do not measure spurious relationships with variables such as learning disabilities phenomena and test anxiety? Is it even possible? How do policymakers reconcile this dilemma?

3. What do administrators and state department officials emphasize most: coverage of everything in the textbook or academic performance as measured on state tests?

4. We are trying to make sure that there are no loopholes in our policies as we implement our standards-based system. Can you direct me to a district that has "teaching to standards as a non-negotiable" in its board/district governing policies?

5. How do you implement standards without spending hours working on plans? Can you recommend some resources on this subject?

6. As we work with the idea of Power Standards, I hear teachers express the concern that there are parts of the content that need to be introduced and explored at a grade level in order for the students to meet the Power Standards at the next grade level. These introduced and explored areas don't seem to be coming through in the Power Standards, yet are necessary for student success over time. Are we missing something in the process of determining Power Standards or in the interpretation of the intent?

7. Some teachers claim that universities will never stand for a standards-based education approach because they need GPAs, class ranks, valedictorians, etc. We already know of the PASS program in Oregon, but are there any other examples of universities preferring or allowing the SBE approach?

8. What is the balance between asking a district to start from scratch in identifying standards and creating assessments, and handing the district a "best of" list of standards and assessments? I understand that the collaborative efforts of a district's staff will gain greater buy-in as well as an increased level of sustainability, but it strikes me that there would be some standards that have proven to be "timeless" and "borderless."

9. I've been asked by my district to help create Power Standards for the visual arts. My dilemma is that there are only five visual arts content standards. Are Power Standards really necessary if there are only five standards to begin with and the five standards are pretty clear?

10. I believe our "standards" are actually "do" lists and so complicated, long, and repetitive that they scare teachers away. Is there an example available of what "Power Standards" might look like and what benchmarks might be at a particular grade level?

11. You specifically talked about cutting the 6th grade math standards from over eighty down to seven essential standards. Have you done this with all subjects in all grade levels? If you have, is this information published somewhere and how can we get it? What were the seven standards for the 6th grade math program? We have teachers doing report cards by going through a check-off system of every standard a child has met. So far, this has only affected the elementary level, but the middle school is next for the same process. I'm a special education teacher and I know how paperwork takes away from the time it takes to prepare to teach. There has to be a better way.

12. I am trying to answer staff questions regarding the Power Standards we heard you speak about. I believe you stated there are six Power Standards that have twenty-five years worth of research. Can you assist in the efforts of locating these identified Power Standards?

13. Can you recommend some resources to help me convince my colleagues that it is better to measure students against a standard than against each other? I am trying to show them that standards-based education is our best option to improve student achievement, but they are demanding proof.

14. I remember that you mentioned a study that showed pretty convincingly that teachers who were faced with "mile wide, inch deep" curriculum could actually raise scores on tests designed to test coverage of the curriculum by focusing on the main concepts and teaching them well. This was one of the main points behind the "Power Standards" concept. I would like a reference to this study if I can get one. I want to be able to actually quote it rather than just sharing hearsay.

Chapter 2: Standards-Based Performance Assessment

15. I understand that you are in favor of standardized testing but not the bell curve as a comparative evaluation because of the diversity within. What other means of measurement can we use? As a future administrator, what more can I do?

16. Should I ask my teachers to set measurable goals for each quarter? My hunch is that this would be micro-managing and that they should give assessments with their annual goals in mind, look at the results, celebrate gains in proficiency, and focus on the areas that are causing the most difficulty in the next nine-week period. But I thought I should ask the master. What do you recommend?

17. We want all of our administrators to have the same understanding of what we mean when we talk about common assessment. Could you give us some

recommended readings that we could provide to all of our administrators to give us all a common knowledge base regarding common assessment?

18. What four steps characterize performance assessment and what happens at each step?

19. I have heard of research supporting the value of "dramatic representations" performed by students to demonstrate what they've learned. Is it possible for you to let me know whose research this is?

20. I am looking for a measure that is reliable, fair, and helpful for accountability. I have heard of an entrance and exit exam or evaluation for middle school students specifically. Can you suggest anything?

21. Last year I established benchmarks for each administration of an assessment and measured the percentage of students who met the benchmark. The benchmark changed for each administration of assessment; that is, the mid-year benchmark was 50 percent, while the March benchmark was 70 percent.

    We then measured the percentage of students in each class that met the benchmark.

    Would it be more "valid" to use a 70 percent benchmark for each administration of the tests or would a changing benchmark be better? I found that setting a benchmark was very valuable in monitoring progress, however, in some cases the mid-year "pass rate" per class was considerably higher than the March pass rate (with a higher benchmark.) I wonder if teachers became complacent when the mid-year rate was relatively high, which resulted in a lower "pass rate" in March.

22. We have teachers working on common, frequent curricular assessments to determine student levels of proficiency on identfed "Power Standards" in each grade level and content area. Our next phase will be to begin to develop performance assessments that can provide data that can replace some of these common curricular assessments and to develop a standards-based reporting system for parents.

We have provided the teachers with a suggested assessment format that will ensure that all levels of Bloom's *Taxonomy* are assessed.

Suggested Assessment Format:

• One question on an explanation of their learning

• 2-3 multiple choice

• 2-3 true/false, where the student must underline the part that makes the statement true, and if false, correct it

• One application or scenario problem

Can you give me feedback on this format? In particular, I have a question on the development of the scoring quide that will accompany the assessment. Do you have a recommendation on how teachers should evaluate multiple items on an assessment to determine a student's level of proficiency?

23. Our administration requires us to assess our students weekly and compare their progress to a pacing chart that they have provided for us. Not only do we find it difficult to keep up, but I feel that we are missing out on the bigger picture of actually analyzing our students' true strengths and weaknesses. Do you have any insights?

24. In the process of implementing standards-based education in our high school, we are encountering considerable resistance from teachers regarding relearning and reassessing in the classroom for students who did not achieve proficiency in the initial assessment. We hear all the usual reasons from "it makes my class too easy," to "there is no retaking in real life," and all the other usual excuses. What can I say to them?

25. Does a district-wide assessment destroy building-based work?

26. I am struggling to find a way to assess my students on what they know while helping them achieve more on the state test. Should I give them a multiple choice assessment (because the state test is multiple choice) on capitalization if that is all that has been covered? That way, I would have a better understanding of where the student needs help before proceeding to the next topic. But the other issue is what will

help the students score higher on the state mandated test. I believe that this method would assess where students are at that point in the curriculum, it would assess where teachers may need help, and it would give the superintendent a better idea whether the students are "on target" with the curriculum.

27. How do you know that your company's standards-based performance assessments really work?

28. I am a teacher and I need research backing up your International Performance Assessment System (IPAS). Do you have any resources you may e-mail me or direct me to on the internet?

Chapter 3: Reading and Student Achievement

29. In your book, *Accountability in Action*, you state that increased time on reading in the curriculum can lead to higher test scores in science, even when time spent on science is decreased. I know that some of the high-stakes tests have science components that enable the better readers to succeed because the science information is supplied in a text form. The students can simply glean the information out of the test material to find the correct answer. Our Stanford-9 exams were largely of this sort. This would, of course, enable the better readers to score higher on the exam.

But what of the tests that rely on questions that refer to material that was learned in the classroom and not supplied in the test material? To which of these two kinds of tests does your data refer? Are scores higher even for those tests in which students must know the material prior to taking the test? If so, how can this be?

30. Have you done any research, or do you know of any that has been done, that studies the effect of reading nonfiction (versus reading narrative fiction) on students' vocabulary development? Also, I'm interested in resources on the positive effects that writing non-fiction has on student achievement.

31. Last year, our school began using a new reading program in grades K-3 in an effort to bring all students up to their appropriate grade level in reading and improve our reading scores on the state test. The new program is a Pearson Learning program based on levelled readers, running records, and Direct Reading Assessment (DRA). We use the program along with Accelerated Reader, the STAR (a computerized CLOZE-based placement test), and the Tests for Higher Standards. We believed that all of these components would go together to present a cohesive picture of student achievement. So far, we are getting erratic results on the various assessments, and they do not seem consistent with how the students do on the state test. What can we do to make sure that all of the components are giving us a valid picture of what we need to work on before the students take the state test?

32. Could you please provide me with information regarding silent reading's benefits over oral reading in the classroom? I am making a claim that oral reading is detrimental to the self esteem of children who struggle because they are embarrassed to read in front of a class. I also claim that oral reading tends not to cater to students who have short attention spans. Are these claims valid?

33. We are researching reading programs successfully implemented by high schools to improve student reading comprehension as we attempt to design a program that will work for us. Any ideas on a specific program and/or school I should contact?

34. I am interested in knowing what experience you may have with the Accelerated Reading Program. Accelerated Reader is utilized in grades 3-5 currently. Do you have any data related to its impact on achievement?

35. Do you think Sustained Silent Reading is essential for student success, or is it just an ineffective, unstructured time for students to daydream? I have colleagues that claim that, especially for our more underprivileged kids, it is a waste of time.

36. I am an English teacher at the high school level who has recently been having problems with a new principal. Our new principal states that he questions my assigning fifteen to twenty minutes (out of ninety minutes) of class time to silent reading and doubts it promotes learning. I am in search of information to support silent reading and the positive effects that it creates. If you know of any journal articles or research papers to help me in this "proof" of benefits, please let me know.

37. Recently at a conference I was told there has been new research done on SSR being used in conjunction with writing. I was told that the research shows no gain made in schools using SSR unless there was the component of writing added to the SSR time. Where can I find this research?

38. I find it difficult to have SSR with my 3rd graders. Some just flip through a book and say, "I'm done." Others need to use the bathroom, get a tissue, etc. to try and use up the thirty minutes. Only a few actually read. I am frustrated!

39. How should SSR as a high school-wide initiative be implemented? Does research support reading improvement as a result of SSR? What diagnostic test could be administered before and during the initiative to monitor improvement? Would it be effective for every student in the school to read at the same designated time twenty minutes, twice weekly? How many minutes does research show as being productive? Could the SSR rubric provided in *Making Standards Work* be calculated as a grade?

40. I am looking for practices used with SSR, how the time for SSR might fit into a block schedule, and actual statistics from a school that has actually implemented an SSR program and experienced an increase in reading levels, to support the approval of an SSR program at the high school level. Any help would be appreciated.

41. I am aware of many resources on writing, but specifically wanted resources on reading comprehension and test scores. I understand that you have stressed expository text: reading shorter works such as articles in depth instead of just a lot of longer, fictional novels. Where in your works or articles could I find this information?

42. I am interested in finding research regarding academic content in pre-school and kindergarten as a predictor for reading success. Do you know where I can find this research?

Chapter 4: Writing and Student Achievement

43. I am trying to convince my principal that our students should be required to do some nonfiction writing every day. He says he will only agree to it if I can prove that it will raise test scores, and most of our tests are multiple choice. Do you have any evidence you can supply me with?

44. The Language Arts teachers in my district are confused as to what is meant by "nonfiction writing." For the most part, the elementary and middle school staff thinks of this as anything related to content in reading, math, science, and social studies. This would also include biography and autobiography. The high school staff felt that if the students were reading a fiction piece and then doing research (they called this literary analysis) and read other pieces of information about it and wrote a paper, this was nonfiction writing. My question is: Isn't nonfiction writing related to informational reading and not a piece of fiction? If their literary analysis is written in this format, is that nonfiction writing?

45. Do you have any caveats about middle school field trips in light of the standards movement?

46. Please answer one question for me. If I have limited language arts time is it justified for me to use twenty minutes each day for journal writing that isn't assessed?

47. My principal and I are attempting to "nudge" writing in our school in a positive direction, and we wanted your input.

First, a committee sent out a survey to the entire staff. How much writing is everyone doing, what form does the writing take, how is the writing assessed, and so on? It came as no surprise to me that our results were very positive. We have a good staff and a good school. Writing is happening throughout the building. Now, how do we make it better, and where do we go from here?

The committee has planned a very basic follow-up activity for our upcoming in-service day. Teachers will sit in on their colleagues' classrooms (sans students!) to hear about successful writing strategies, techniques, and procedures that are utilized. The goal is to establish a starting point for discussion, for sharing, and for fostering an atmosphere of academic dialogue among the staff. Your thoughts?

48. I am having discussions with my staff about the increase in non-fiction writing in an elementary setting. We are wondering more specifically, what that would look like? I have downloaded the sample assessments from the websites, but was wondering if there are more sample non-fiction writing activities that we could look at from the 90-90-90 schools.

49. We are looking for research that shows the impact writing has on math achievement. I understand that you have some research supporting the importance of writing and achievement. Do you have articles or research you would be willing to share regarding this topic?

50. The administration has asked us to make sure our students do more writing. Many of the teachers in my school are resistant and feel the "requirements" from the administration are not aligned with their content, and therefore are reluctant to learn and grow. Can you help?

51. Do you have a few tips for high school parents who want to support the school's writing focus at home? I am noting the *Reason to Write* as a possible resource.

52. I encourage my students to turn in a rough draft of any papers I assign so that I can review them and make suggestions for improvement. I am finding it increasingly difficult to get students to revise their rough drafts when I give them back. The general attitude now is, "I did it once, why do I have to do it again?" I have done this quite a bit over the years and I used to see improvement by the end of the school year. Not anymore. Any suggestions?

53. I'm currently working with my teachers on revising their current rubric and taking them through the writing process (what teachers will be doing within the content and what students will be doing). But I'm meeting with resistance and I have a question for you: Which is a stronger practice in writing: having students use the writing process or having students synthesize thinking in a written response (without formally using the writing process)?

54. I would like to develop a writing rubric for my elementary school. I'd like it to end up prominently posted in all classrooms and in the hallways. The communications skills specialist and assistant principal thought it was an interesting idea, but not for the primary grades. They thought it had potential for grades 3, 4, and 5 only. What are your feelings on this?

55. My school is looking at how to measure writing to show growth on a quarterly basis. What would your suggestion be? We would like to get away from using a 4, 3, 2, 1 score as the score may not show growth. For example, a student scores a low 2 on the rubric at the beginning of the 1st quarter, then a high 2 during the next quarter. How is the growth shown? Is this where a narrative is included explaining the score and what that means? How would you show growth in writing on a quarterly basis?

56. We are questioning our assessment process for writing. Presently, we give monthly writing prompts with each prompt being a different genre of writing (personal narrative/persuasive writing). The prompts are not always based on/in content discipline (social studies/science). The question is:

Should writing prompts be a consistent genre of writing (for the year per grade level) and always based on a content area? We are considering making it so that the students will be assessed monthly over the same type of nonfiction writing, with each grade level being responsible for a form of writing to ensure understanding (ex: 6th grade would do a research form, 5th grade persuasive, 4th grade personal narrative, etc.). What do you think?

57. I have heard you speak of research studies that were related to writing performance mitigating the impact of poverty. You also advocated a large literacy block with a focus on the writing process. Might you share with me those particular studies in full or refer me to the site where I might obtain them?

58. What articles and books would you recommend that I use with building principals to make the case for the implementation of a nonfiction, across-the-curriculum writing program? I would prefer to show my principals the value of such a program through research.

59. I would like to see research & citations for the data regarding achievement and nonfiction writing. I need that research and those sources. It is crucial to a 6-district in service we're holding soon. I appreciate any help you can give me.

Chapter 5: Classroom Issues

60. I am wondering if you can point me toward research that supports the importance of looping at the high school level. I am working to foster the importance of relationships as connected to learning by keeping kids with teachers for two years within particular classes.

61. I have heard you mention the concept of a "welcome center" for new students. Our school has a large amount of student mobility and I am looking for ways to cope with it. Can you give me any ideas?

62. The practice at my building has been to test students at the 5th and 6th grade level and ability group them for math in groups such as low 5th grade math, regular 5th grade math, 6th grade math and 7th grade math. I have found some research that supports not grouping low students for instruction in academic areas. I believe that you have stated that students should be taught at their grade level and the time altered to meet their needs. Should all of the low students be put together and be taught at a slow pace or do the students benefit from their peers that are more successful at math? Is there some research I can present to my teachers to show them that we should not put all of the low students together or should we continue this practice?

63. We are being told to teach at grade level no matter what the students' abilities are. We have many 8th grade students with 6th grade-level math and reading skills, yet we are told not to teach to their current level, but rather teach to their grade level. May I have your opinion on this?

64. When discussing mixed ability grouping, you outline the benefits of a standards-based education both for students performing at high level and a low level of proficiency. But in the classroom, what happens to the middle-level students? How do teachers challenge and engage the students who demonstrate proficiency after a few tries, therefore not needing assistance from their peers, but also not strong enough (or willing, for that matter) to teach others? I assume the answer to my question lies somewhere in between the approaches for low and high level performers, but I was curious how it really played out in the real world.

65. I am the AP of a middle school, and our district has been implementing differentiated instruction for the past two years. Most of our staff is using differentiated lessons, but we are getting questions about assessing the different groups in the classroom. The one question which keeps coming up is, "How do I justify the grades for groups which are doing easier work?" If you could give some suggestions or ideas that I can share with my staff, I would appreciate it.

66. I am an ESL teacher for K-5. We are moving to inclusion rather than pullout, although we still pull out for newcomers to the U.S. for their first year and give intensive English instruction. Please direct me to the research and methodology that is employed by the 90/90/90 schools, or any information relevant to teaching second language learners. I am wondering if there is a specific standard that must be reached before the student benefits more from inclusion than pullout.

67. Are there effective resources or best practices in the area of writing to deal with a significantly large ESL population?

68. I need some research and information on the increased achievement for non-severely disabled special education students in a standards-based environment. Can you assist me with this?

69. We are revamping our 3rd, 4th, and 5th grade after-school remedial program in an attempt to raise scores on our state test. We have many 3rd graders who did not pass the test who will retake it in the spring as 4th graders. We have many 5th graders who did not pass it in the 3rd or 4th grade.

Where should we start the benchmark? The teachers will need to know where to begin with the students because many children will not be with their daily teacher for the extra help.

Monitoring the students' progress is a must. There will be so many different levels and needs, I am not sure where to begin. I want success for the students to improve our overall scores. Can you help?

70. I have two classes of 6th grade language arts/social studies in a block schedule, which I love. My classes are typical because they have students who can and will, and students who can and won't, and students who are working to their ability, but their ability level is low. How many opportunities do I give to students to meet the standard before moving on to the next standard? Some standards in language arts can be ongoing, but in social studies, our time for the standards covering Egypt, Kush, and Mesopotamia is only about three

to four weeks. An "inch wide and a mile deep" is a great idea, but at some point, the classes need to move forward, perhaps leaving some students behind. What are your thoughts?

71. I am principal of a public high school where my predecessor resigned because she was asked to implement honors classes at the 9th and 10th grade levels, which she objected to as a return to tracking. I don't want to see a return to rigid tracking either. However, I'm not sure that there isn't a small percentage of kids who are so advanced in their academic skills that they need something different.

    Many of my progressive friends believe that tracking is bad, but few can really explain how we can have 10th graders in the same class who read from 3rd grade to 12th grade level and not have someone's needs not addressed. I'm actually most worried that the teenager who reads like the 3rd grader is the one who gets left behind. It seems meeting standards means groupings have to be different sometimes, and we just need to make sure boundaries are fluid and not hard. What are your thoughts on this subject?

72. Can you please help me to locate research that shows the link between achievement and increased self-esteem?

73. I'm looking for information on attendance issues in the classroom. We want to use this to present to parents with elementary children who have started to show troubling patterns of attendance. Do you know of a "critical" number of absences that begins to impact achievement?

74. I have trouble getting K–5 teachers to understand the reason for homework, and more importantly, the reason for NO HOMEWORK. Please help me with some examples or articles to support the real reasons for homework or a lack thereof.

Chapter 6: Grading and Reporting Data

75. At our elementary school, the policy on math problems is to take off 2 points per problem if students don't include the "label." This means if the student doesn't write the word "tickets" in a problem asking how many tickets were sold, they are docked two points. Their grade can go from a passing grade to a failing one if they don't label all the problems. The teachers do not, however, give partial credit for including the "label" if the student gets the math wrong but writes the label correctly. They say that taking off for the labels is an important part of "following directions," but our report cards have a separate conduct grade for "listens and follows directions." What are your thoughts on this?

76. I have heard it said that averaging a student's grade with a zero in it for missing work is somewhat harsh, because they have such a deficit to come up from. It seems that if a 50 were assigned to an F it would be easier to bring that grade up, or perhaps a fairer place to start in the averaging process. Should missing assignments still get zeros since nothing was turned in, or should they be assigned an F with a standard percentage so the student is not so far down in the hole that he can't get out?

77. I have heard you speak of the inconsistency in using the 4 point GPA and the 100 percent scale as measures. I am not able to explain this to a fellow teacher. Could you help me with this?

78. My school is interested in introducing and eventually establishing a "No Failure Policy" that allows students to reach mastery level in all subject levels. As we begin this process, it would be extremely helpful if you could provide us with examples of high schools currently utilizing this approach.

79. We have a standards-based report card that measures students' progress against an end-of-the-year expectation. One of the problems we struggle with is showing progress

for the earlier grading periods. A "2" for "Progressing Toward End-of-Year Standard" could mean that the student does not yet have the skills or understanding expected by the end of the year OR it could mean that part of the standard has not yet been taught. How do we address end-of-year vs. current progress?

80. I need some clarification. If I am going to look at a cohort over the past four years of testing, my understanding is that I should only look at those students who have remained in our schools for the past four years.

   For example, if the 2nd grade enrollment is 250 students, the 3rd grade enrollment 225, the 4th grade enrollment 250, and the 5th grade enrollment 250, then the cohort for all four years should be the 150 students that have remained with us for the whole four years.

   The person who did my job before me looked at cohorts for the past four years by looking at all the scores over four years, not respective of the transience of the number of children who came and left. Which is the most accurate when looking for trends? Any assistance would be appreciated.

81. We want to disaggregate student performance data for the past three years based on Free and Reduced Lunch status, as well as Limited English Proficiency and Special Education. Is it typical to compare each subgroup to the whole (i.e., all students) or to all students minus that subgroup? In other words, should I compare F&R students to all students, or to Paid Lunch students (which is essentially another subgroup)? If comparing them to all students, the F&R students are represented in both data sets. I ask primarily for graphing purposes, but my graphs will influence how the board and administration make data-driven decisions. Can you help?

82. Regarding district-wide or school-wide summary growth data, what represents a statistically significant gain? For example, at School A, 77 percent of 3rd graders were proficient in reading in the fall, while 83 percent were proficient come spring. In School B, the fall figure was 88

percent proficient and spring was 90 percent proficient. Did either or both schools make statistically significant gains? Is there a formula or rule of thumb? Does it depend on "n" count?

In the past we have been happy to report "gains at all schools/all grades/all subjects." Now we want to better characterize those gains. Any ideas?

83. I need to test a hypothesis. I believe that more time spent with a particular curriculum program has resulted in higher vocabulary scores, but I would like to be able to back it up with proof. My question is, what do I ask teachers?

1. How much time each week have you spent on the program?

2. How many words do you currently have on your word wall?

3. How do you transfer the word wall into instruction?

4. How many days a week do you actually do the program?

5. In looking at your lesson plans, how many total days did you work with words?

Should I ask all of these questions? If my hypothesis is correct, I should see higher vocabulary scores in those classes that actually implemented the program block at a higher level. Any feedback or suggestions would be greatly appreciated. I am looking forward to see if I can substantiate my FEELING about this!

Chapter 7: Successful Schools: 90/90/90 and Beyond

84. In my district, the 90/90/90 studies are currently resurfacing as a topic of interest. Is there additional research since your original study?

85. I would like to know where I can find a list of California 90/90/90 schools. I have seen it referenced in various articles, but I

have not been able to find the list itself. Also, what were the criteria for meeting the 90 percent achievement?

86. I am teaching developmentally disabled children and I feel that I am being given inappropriate directives and unreasonable expectations from my administrators, all in the name of higher expectations and the 90/90/90 research. So, have you thrown out the bell curve and decided that all children have exactly the same intelligence and that therefore intelligence does not matter? If that is the case, then are my children who have IQs of between 55 and 69 expected to learn in regular class as if they really have IQs of 100 as does every other child? Could you advise me as to what you tell teachers of developmentally disabled children? I need to talk to my administrators.

87. I am interested in sources about urban high schools with over 2000 students, ethnically diverse, and high-poverty populations that are successfully reaching high standards. Can you help me?

88. Can you refer me to any 90/90/90 middle schools or high schools? Most of what I have read about 90/90/90 schools is in reference to elementary schools. We have three high schools in our district with high poverty, high minority numbers, and we are hoping to visit similar high schools experiencing high academic achievement.

89. As a new school (this is our inaugural year) whose students already have high test scores, I believe we have a real opportunity to lay a strong foundation with our school improvement plan and the process of making that plan. Can you give me some advice or suggest books or research we might use to guide our process? I would like to base the creation of our team and the subsequent school improvement plan on a proven system.

    In researching through my own library, I have spent some time with Marzano's *What Works in Schools*. Would you suggest this work for a book study by the school improvement team? Do you have other suggestions?

90. Our public junior high is contemplating going to an "academy" style school. Where can I find good sources of "schools that work" and "best practices?" Our teachers will be able to design our own plan and we need help dreaming of the possible and thinking outside the box. What awesome ideas are going on out there that we could implement?

91. What private schools in New England are considered to be the very best in regard to standards and student achievement? What practices do they have in place to ensure the students become proficient in the standards? I would like the names of the schools, as we would like to contact each of them regarding their standards and practices.

92. Could you please email to us your definition of "academic"? We are hoping to clear up the concerns that have arisen and are threatening to impede the progress and acceptance of standards-based education here at our school.

93. In your opinion, what should be the elements of a middle school schedule that best support standards, assessment, and achievement?

94. Would you ever suggest blocks of time for grades K-8 for content areas, especially math and literacy? We are thinking of introducing a ninety-minute-per-day math/literacy block for elementary grades.

95. As assistant superintendent in an elementary district, I am quite interested in using some of the strategies related to "90/90/90 schools," high-poverty and minority schools that are also high-achieving. However, I have found no specific descriptions of the programs in those schools and no references to the original research. Can you provide citations or refer me to the schools that participated in the studies?

Chapter 8: Uniting Stakeholders for Student Achievement

96. What is your perspective on George Bush's No Child Left Behind Act and how it relates to Title I?

97. How are you able to derive a national standard from a state test?

98. Here in California, there is a theme of conversation associated with the levels of challenge and expectations in the state's curriculum content standards. Has anyone done an analysis to align the comparable rigor of standards across the states? If California's standards are "more rigorous," then we have some reason to understand why in some states in the nation there is a report that no students are "below proficient." Can you help direct me to this kind of answer/information?

99. I am non-instructional personnel, in the Information Technology Department, and feel like I have little input. The information discussed by the majority of educators is not filtered down to us, so we end up making decisions that do not concur with the faculty, nor they with ours. I was wondering what methods or practices you can suggest that would bridge that gap. Perhaps it is a common problem that has no solutions, but I feel I could provide valuable information and tactics if given the opportunity. What are your thoughts?

100. I would like to try a school-wide focus for professional development this year rather than have each teacher write an individual professional goal. Does this sound reasonable? What focus areas would have the greatest impact? Our test scores overall have been below the district for last spring. I would like a school-wide focus on reading and assessment.

101. Our district is asking our teachers to follow a "pacing plan" by which all of the teachers must teach the same lessons the same day the entire school year. There is very little wiggle room in this plan. What are your thoughts on this?

102. I am the principal at a high school where my staff is difficult to change. Sometimes they think they know it all. However, last month, we reviewed our school data and talked in groups about what the word "proficient" means to them. We will then discuss student work (shuffled, with names removed) and try to agree on a definition of proficiency so that we can all tell whether our students are meeting standards.

What am I missing here? How can I be more structured so when the teachers look at the student samples they know exactly what to look for and what to do?

103. I am dealing with a group of high school teachers who are very angry about having to do some collaboratively-scored writing and reading assessments. They see it as "teaching to the test" and have even gone so far as to write an open letter in the local papers claiming that the central office is taking all of the creativity out of the classroom by doing this work. I will be meeting with this staff soon and would love to have some of your research at my fingertips. Could you please let me know where I can get my hands on the appropriate studies or other possible sources?

104. I am considering implementing a "family support scale" to be used in understanding some of the antecedents of test performance. Can I get some suggestions for this scale to use with the parents in my district?

105. How do you communicate the standards to the parents?

Appendix B:
Standards Implementation Checklists

Classroom Checklist

	Professional Practice	Exemplary	Proficient	Progressing	Remarks
1.	Standards are highly visible in the classroom. The standards are expressed in language that the students understand.				
2.	Examples of "exemplary" student work are displayed throughout the classroom.				
3.	Students can spontaneously explain what "proficient" work means for each assignment.				
4.	For every assignment, project, or test, the teacher publishes in advance the explicit expectations for "proficient" work.				
5.	Student evaluation is always done according to the standards and scoring guide criteria and *never* done based on a "curve."				
6.	The teacher can explain to any parent or other stakeholder the specific expectations of students for the year.				
7.	The teacher has the flexibility to vary the length and quantity of curriculum content on a day to day basis in order to insure that students receive more time on the most critical subjects.				
8.	Commonly used standards, such as those for written expression, are reinforced in every subject area. In other words, "spelling always counts" —even in math, science, music and every other discipline.				

Classroom Checklist (continued)

	Professional Practice	Exemplary	Proficient	Progressing	Remarks
9.	The teacher has created at least one standards-based performance assessment in the past month.				
10.	The teacher exchanges student work (accompanied by a scoring guide) with a colleague for review and evaluation at least once every two weeks.				
11.	The teacher provides feedback to students and parents about the quality of student work compared to the standards—not compared to other students.				
12.	The teacher helps to build a community consensus in the classroom and with other stakeholders for standards and high expectations of all students.				
13.	The teacher uses a variety of assessment tecyhniques, including (but not limited to) extended written responses, in all disciplines.				
	Other professional practices appropriate for your classroom:				

School Checklist

	Professional Practice	Exemplary	Proficient	Progressing	Remarks
1.	A Standards/Class matrix (standards across the top, classes on the left side) is in a prominent location. Each box indicates the correspondence between a class and the standards. Faculty members and school leaders discuss areas of overlap and standards that are not sufficiently addressed.				
2.	Standards are visible throughout the school and in every classroom.				
3.	The school leaders use every opportunity for parent communication to build a community consensus for rigorous standards and high expectations for all students.				
4.	Information about rigorous standards and high expectations is a specific part of the agenda of every faculty meeting, site council meeting, and parent organization meeting.				
5.	The principal personally evaluates some student projects or papers compared to a school-wide or district-wide standard.				
6.	The principal personally evaluates selected student portfolios compared to a school-wide or district-wide standard.				
7.	Examples of "exemplary" student papers are highly visible.				
8.	Job interview committees explicitly inquire about the views of a candidate about standards, performance assessment, and instructional methods for helping all students achieve high standards.				

Professional Practice	Exemplary	Proficient	Progressing	Remarks
9. A "jump-start" program is available to enhance the professional education of new teachers who do not have an extensive background in standards and assessment techniques.				
10. Every discretionary dollar spent on staff development and instructional support is specifically linked to student achievement, high standards, and improved assessment.				
11. Faculty meetings are used for structured collaboration with a focus on student work - not for the making of announcements.				
12. The principal personally reviews the assessment and instructional techniques used by teachers as part of the personnel review and evaluation process. The principal specifically considers the link between teacher assessments and standards.				
Other professional practices appropriate for your school:				

District/State/System Checklist

Professional Practice	Exemplary	Proficient	Progressing	Remarks
1. The system has an accountability plan that is linked to student achievement of standards - not to the competition of schools with one another.				
2. The system has a program for monitoring the "antecedents of excellence" - that is, the strategies that schools use to achieve high standards. The monitoring system does not depend on test scores alone.				
3. The system explicitly authorizes teachers to modify the curriculum guides in quantity and emphasis so that student needs for core academic requirements in math, science, language arts and social studies are met.				
4. The system publishes the "best practices in standards-based assessment" on an annual basis, recognizing the creative efforts of teachers and administrators.				
5. The system has established an assessment task force to monitor the implementation of effective and fair assessments, and to distribute models of educational assessments for use throughout the year.				
6. The system provides timely feedback on district-level assessments so that all assessments can be used to inform instruction during the current school year. Assessments that are not used for the purpose of informing instruction and improving student achievement are not used.				

District/State/System Checklist (continued)

Professional Practice	Exemplary	Proficient	Progressing	Remarks
7. The system reports to the public a comprehensive set of student achievement results throughout the year.				
8. The system uses multiple methods of assessments for system-wide assessments. It never relies on a single indicator or single assessment method to represent student achievement.				
9. There is a clearly identified senior leader at the system level who is responsible for standards, assessment, and accountability, and who communicates this information clearly to all stakeholders.				
10. Commitment to standards is a criteria in all hiring decisions at all levels.				
11. The system monitors the investment of resources - including staff development, technology, and capital expenditures - for a consistent and clear link to student achievement of standards. System leaders can provide explicit examples of changes in resource allocation decisions that reflect this commitment.				
12. Evaluations of schools and of building leaders are based on student achievement - not based on competition or any other norm-referenced system.				

District/State/System Checklist (continued)

Professional Practice	Exemplary	Proficient	Progressing	Remarks
13. The system does not take into account ethnicity and socio-economic level in determining its expectations of student performance. These variables, along with linguistic background, learning disabilities, and other factors, are included in resource allocation decisions and the development of instructional and assessment strategies.				
14. The system allocates resources based on student needs and a commitment to the opportunity for all students to achieve standards. Resources are not allocated merely on the basis of student population - the objective is equity of opportunity, not equality of distribution.				
Other professional practices appropriate for your system:				

Appendix C:
How to Identify Power Standards

> Note: The information in this appendix has been adapted, with permission, from *Power Standards: Identifying the Standards that Matter the Most* by Larry Ainsworth.

Theory is always important for establishing a purpose for activity. But after the rationale for developing Power Standards has been presented and the group has had time to discuss the ideas and issues raised, it is time to put theory into practice. In this chapter, I will share the Center for Performance Assessment process that individual schools and entire school systems around the country have effectively followed to develop their agreed-upon collection of Power Standards.

Determine Power Standards Identification Criteria

Let us revisit the two sets of suggested criteria for identifying the Power Standards presented at the end of Chapter One.
1. Endurance
2. Leverage
3. Readiness for next level of learning

The second set is derived from the guiding question: *"What do your students need for success—in school (this year, next year, and so on), in life, and on your state tests?"*
1. School
2. Life
3. State Test

Rather than seeing the two sets as distinctly different from one another, the following sentence shows how they can be combined into a revised guiding question for identifying Power Standards:

> *"What do your students need for success—in school this year, next year, and so on (leverage; readiness for next levels of learning), in life (endurance), and on your state tests?"*

To focus discussions and help participants agree upon the selection of Power Standards, consider using also the other two guiding questions that were presented in the "Punt the Rhombus" illustration in Chapter One:

1. What essential understandings and skills do our students need?

2. Which standards and/or indicators can be clustered or incorporated into others?

Determine which criteria and guiding questions to use as you prepare to begin the Power Standards identification process.

Beginning the Process

Each of the steps detailed below can be initially accomplished in one full-day workshop. For simplicity's sake, I will present the process for identifying Power Standards in *one* content area only. However, they can be identified in several content areas simultaneously by having representative educators from each separate content area seated together and following the process described below.

When working with a K-12 group, I begin by asking participants to **select the content area** in which they would first like to identify their Power Standards. I then ask everyone to **sit in one of four grade-span groups**, usually K-2, 3-5, 6-8, or 9-12. I encourage everyone present—classroom educators, administrators, curriculum specialists, and all others—to select the grade span they know the best in this particular content area.

To keep the task at hand from becoming overwhelming or unwieldy, I ask everyone to **select a particular section of the content area standards** in which to begin the process. For example, the content area of language arts has four domains: reading, writing, listening, and speaking. Rather than try and identify the Power Standards in all four domains simultaneously, I urge them to select one of the four. After successfully identifying the Power Standards for that first selected domain, groups repeat the same process with the remaining three.

The same can be done in mathematics, where there are typically six or seven math strands. Everyone can begin with one particular strand, such as Number Sense, for example, and then repeat the same process later with the other remaining strands.

The next step is for each grade-span group to **select one grade within their grade span** in which to begin. I ask participants to open their chosen subject matter standards, turn to the one grade they have selected, and **find the one particular section** they decided to start with.

I remind participants to **keep in mind whichever agreed-upon identification criteria they selected** as they complete the first activity. I write their selected criteria and guiding questions on the overhead projector, chalkboard, or on a PowerPoint slide so that they are visible to everyone in the room as they work through the process.

Then I direct the groups to *take the next five minutes and on their own quickly mark* each standard and indicator for this section that *they* consider to be **absolutely essential** for student success in the grade selected. I ask them to please wait to talk to colleagues sitting next to them until after they have finished.

"Just check the ones you think students must know and be able to do, the ones that you consider to be non-negotiable. As you find ones that you're not sure about, mark them quickly with a question mark and move on down the list. Ready? Please begin."

The group sets to work, and the room is silent as people engage in the task. When the five minutes have elapsed, I call the group back together and ask them, "Why am I giving you so little time for something so important? Why not give you ten, fifteen, even twenty minutes to do this?"

Invariably, the response is, "We'd end up with everything checked, and we'd be right back where we started, with too much!"

And that's exactly the point. The longer we think about each one, the more standards we mark, since the standards represent a comprehensive list of the knowledge and skills we want all students to learn in a deep and meaningful way. But if we consider again the notion that not all standards and indicators are equal in importance, and the fact that there are simply not enough days in the school year to teach all of them in an "inch wide, mile deep" manner, then it is clear that we need to prioritize the standards according to the criteria decided. This quick marking of the standards will greatly assist educators in the first step of this prioritization process.

Table Talk

"Now I'd like you to **talk to your colleagues** at the table. Share the standards and indicators that you marked with each other, and note where you agree, where you disagree, where you're not sure. What about the ones with a question mark? Did you cluster or incorporate any standards and indicators into others? If you or one of your colleagues does not have a standard or indicator marked that you consider essential, did s/he see that particular one as being part of another standard that you both selected? The goal is to **reach an initial consensus** of what the Power Standards should be for this particular grade in this particular section."

The room now comes alive with animated conversation as participants **compare their choices and note similarities and differences**. While this discussion is taking place, I walk around the room and listen in on the conversations. Often, what I hear is easy agreement. When there is a difference of opinion, it usually has to do with an individual's different interpretation of what the standard means. One educator will say to another, "I didn't pick that particular standard or indicator because I saw it as being incorporated into this other one." In other words, through discussion, what initially appeared as disagreement was, in fact, merely a different interpretation. In general, educators usually agree on what they deem important for students to learn. They are able to justify their choices with logic and from experience.

When the group as a whole has finished this step in the process, I bring them back together to provide directions for the next step.

Consult Testing Information Guides

Most states provide educators with printed information on either their Department of Education website or in booklet form that describes the type and frequency of questions students will encounter on the actual state assessment. For states using a norm-referenced or criterion-referenced test from a commercial publisher, a testing information guide is often included with the purchased testing materials. Examples of this include the *Stanford 9 Compendium of Tested Skills and Objectives* (Harcourt) and the *CTBS Teacher's Guide to TerraNova* (McGraw-Hill). These documents can be an invaluable tool for identifying Power Standards and need to be made available to participants at this stage of the process, if at all possible. (Note: Testing Information Guides may not be available for individual purchase. Educators may wish to inquire as to the availability of these from their district's central office.)

Consult District or State Test Data

If no such information is available or if this information does not provide enough specificity regarding the concepts and skills tested, utilize school or district item analysis reports of the state test data to inform the Power Standards identification process. This data will provide insights into the type and frequency of items tested. Those standards and indicators that reflect these tested items can then be identified so that participants can decide whether or not they need to be included in their Power Standards based on the frequency of their representation on the state test.

At this point I say to the group, "On this first pass that you've just completed, you prioritized the standards and indicators based on your own opinion and experience. Now, let's spend the next 15 to 30 minutes and *refer to your state's Testing Information Guides and/or your available test data* to see which concepts and skills will be emphasized the most in terms of the number of questions asked. See if the standards and indicators you just selected are the same ones that the state or the test publisher emphasizes the most. *Revise your selections* accordingly on your individual team lists."

Chart Selections for Individual Grades

When the groups have finished revising their lists for the particular grades they are working on, I ask them to **record the identifying numbers and letters** of their selected Power Standards and indicators **on pieces of chart-size paper** labeled with specific grades. Rather than copy the full text of each standard and indicator selected, I suggest they write a synopsis or brief phrase after each number and letter that summarizes the content of the ones selected. This will be helpful for later steps in the process.

Discussing Vertical Alignment

"Great! Now, please put your individual grade charts aside for now. Those of you in the classroom, how often are you able to meet and collaborate with colleagues *within* your own grade or department?"

The responses from the group usually indicate once a week or once a month for grade-level or department meetings.

"How often do you meet and collaborate with colleagues in the grades *below and above* your own?"

Wherever I ask this question, the answer is almost always the same: "Never."

"Would it be helpful for you, as you identify your Power Standards, to collaborate in vertical teams in order to identify the ones for the grades immediately before and after your own?"

"Absolutely!"

The Wayne Township "Safety Net"

"Then I'd like to show you what educators in the Metropolitan School District of Wayne Township, a large district in Indianapolis, Indiana, produced by collaborating with teaching colleagues in the grades above and below their own. They identified their K-12 essential knowledge and skills (Power Standards) from their state language arts standards, which they named their 'Safety Net,' and then produced these cards for each grade."

I hold up a colorful set of 8½ x 11 inch laminated cards for everyone to see.

"On the front of this particular card for grade seven are listed the seven language arts *standards* in Indiana. Under each standard is the one *indicator* that their educators determined is critical for seventh grade students to attain. Now look what's on the back!"

I turn the card over to reveal the identified "Safety Nets" for grades 6 and 8. Invariably, there is audible admiration from the audience as people immediately recognize the value of what Wayne Township has created. An example of this two-sided card appears on the next two pages, reprinted with permission.

I continue with my explanation.

"Recognizing the need not only to identify the 'Safety Net' for each grade but to vertically align each grade's selections with the grades above and below, Wayne Township knew it was absolutely necessary to provide time for educators to have cross-grade discussions in order to make those determinations. Once the 'Safety Nets' were vertically aligned *within* each individual grade span, their final step was to vertically align all four grade spans. The result was a K-12 language arts 'Safety Net' that has been produced on these laminated cards and distributed to everyone."

Wayne Township has replicated the same process under the direction of their district curriculum coordinators in mathematics, social studies, science, foreign language, and physical education. All educators in the district receive the "Safety Net" card(s) for the particular content areas they teach.

Wayne Township deliberately identified very few indicators for each content area. Since all K-12 educators have been involved in the process, the expectation is that each educator at every grade level will assume "instructional responsibility" for the particular indicators identified for that grade. In this way, educators can indeed teach their "assigned" indicators for depth of student understanding and continue to build on those indicators introduced in prior grades. This will minimize the necessity to re-teach in subsequent years those indicators that students were expected to learn in earlier years.

Chapter Four describes in full the process Wayne Township followed to identify their Power Standards in each of the content areas listed above. Each of their curriculum coordinators has contributed individual commentaries for this book describing how they received input from all educators in the district as part of their process. Copies of the Wayne Township "Safety Nets" are continually requested by school systems across the nation as a model to guide their own Power Standards identification. Wayne Township administrators have generously allowed me to share their website address in Chapter Four for the benefit of readers who wish to review and download their "Safety Nets" as illustrations of their process.

Grade Below and Grade Above

With the stage set for determining vertical alignment, I lead the group through the next step in the process.

"Let's look again at your just-selected Power Standards for the grade you started with. Now you need to *repeat the same process for both the grade below and the grade above*. On your own, spend a few minutes marking the standards and indicators you think are Power Standards for the grade below the one you just completed. Then compare and contrast your list with your colleagues and revise the list based on the Test Information Guide and/or your test data. Reach initial consensus and record your selections on another sheet of chart-size paper. Then repeat the process one more time with the grade above the one you started with. When this is accomplished, we will be ready to discuss vertical alignment."

The groups start buzzing with activity and before long the grade-span charts are completed.

Looking for the Vertical 'Flow'

"Next we'll look for the vertical alignment between the grades within your own grade span. If you will please *post your three grade-level charts on the wall in order*, beginning with K-2 on the far left, followed by 3-5, and so on, we can *look for the vertical flow within and between the grade spans*."

**MSD WAYNE TWP.
SAFETY NET
CURRICULUM**

Safety Net Skills for
Language Arts Standards

GRADE 7

Standard 1 – Word Recognition, Fluency, and Vocabulary Development

7.1.3 – Clarify word meanings through the use of definition, example, restatement, or through the use of contrast stated in the text.

Standard 2 – Reading Comprehension

7.2.3 – Analyze text that uses the cause-and-effect organizational pattern.

Standard 3 – Literary Response and Analysis

7.3.2 – Identify events that advance the plot and determine how each event explains past or present action or foreshadows (provides clues to) future action.

Standard 4 – Writing Process

7.4.2 – Create an organizational structure that balances all aspects of the composition and uses effective transitions between sentences to unify important ideas.

Standard 5 – Writing Applications (Different Types of Writing and Their Characteristics)

7.5.7 – Write for different purposes and to a specific audience or person, adjusting style and tone as necessary.

Standard 6 – Written English Language Conventions

7.6.8 – Use correct capitalization.

Standard 7 – Listening and Speaking

7.7.4 – Arrange supporting details, reasons, descriptions, and examples effectively.

MSD WAYNE TWP. SAFETY NET CURRICULUM — GRADE 8

Standard 1 – Word Recognition, Fluency, and Vocabulary Development

8.1.1 – Analyze idioms and comparisons, such as analogies, metaphors, and similes, to infer the literal and figurative meanings of phrases.

Standard 2 – Reading Comprehension

8.2.4 – Compare the original text to a summary to determine whether the summary accurately describes the main ideas, includes important details, and conveys the underlying meaning.

Standard 3 – Literary Response and Analysis

8.3.6 – Identify significant literary devices, such as metaphor, symbolism, dialect, and irony, which define a writer's style and use those elements to interpret the work.

Standard 4 – Writing Process

8.4.2 – Create compositions that have a clear message, a coherent thesis (a statement of position on the topic), and end with a clear and well-supported conclusion.

Standard 5 – Writing Applications

8.5.1 – Write biographies, autobiographies, and short stories that:
- tell about an incident, event, or situation using well-chosen details.
- reveal the significance of, or the writer's attitude about, the subject.
- use narrative and descriptive strategies, including relevant dialogue, specific action, physical description, background description, and comparison or contrast of characters.

Standard 6 – Written English Language Conventions

8.6.1 – Use correct and varied sentence types (simple, compound, complex, and compound-complex) and sentence openings to present a lively and effective personal style.

Standard 7 – Listening and Speaking

8.7.12 – Deliver research presentations that:
- define a thesis (a position on the topic).
- research important ideas, concepts, and direct quotations from significant information sources and paraphrase and summarize important perspectives on the topic.
- use a variety of research sources and distinguish the nature and value of each.
- present information on charts, maps, and graphs.

MSD WAYNE TWP. SAFETY NET CURRICULUM — GRADE 6

Standard 1 – Word Recognition, Fluency, and Vocabulary Development

6.1.2 – Identify and interpret figurative language (including similes, comparisons that use like or as, and metaphors, implied comparisons) and words with multiple meanings.

Standard 2 – Reading Comprehension

6.2.4 – Clarify an understanding of texts by creating outlines, notes, diagrams, summaries, or reports.

Standard 3 – Literary Response and Analysis

6.3.6 – Identify and analyze features of themes conveyed through characters, actions, and images.

Standard 4 – Writing Process

6.4.3 – Write informational pieces of several paragraphs that:
- engage the interest of the reader.
- state a clear purpose.
- develop a topic with supporting details and precise language.
- conclude with a detailed summary linked to the purpose of the composition.

Standard 5 – Writing Applications

6.5.2 – Write descriptions, explanations, comparison and contrast papers, and problem and solution essays that: state the thesis (purpose on the topic) or purpose; explain the situation; organize the composition clearly; offer evidence to support arguments and conclusions.

Standard 6 – Written English Language Conventions

6.6.1 – Use simple sentences, compound sentences, and complex sentences; use effective coordination and subordination of ideas, including both main ideas and supporting ideas in single sentences, to express complete thoughts.

Standard 7 – Listening and Speaking

6.7.3 – Restate and carry out multiple-step oral instructions and directions.

The 13 individual grade-level charts go up, and I inform the participants that in a few minutes, I'll ask one or more members from each grade span group to stand next to the charts and provide for the entire K-12 group a brief narrative about their identified Power Standards and what they discovered while working through the selection process. But first I want to provide them all with a focus for listening to each group's sharing, as described in the next section.

Gaps, Overlaps, and Omissions

In assisting school systems in the development of curriculum maps, Heidi Hayes Jacobs, president of Curriculum Designers, Inc., uses a series of terms, "gaps, overlaps, and omissions" to ensure that curriculum is not heavily repeated or inadvertently omitted from one grade to another (1997).

In the identification of Power Standards, it is also particularly important at this step to *look for and identify any gaps, overlaps, and omissions*. Is there a particular standard or indicator needing to be taught to students in more than one grade that is missing from a particular grade's list (a gap)? Is there a certain standard or indicator that is being redundantly taught in two or three grades that could be thoroughly taught in only one grade (an overlap)? Is there a particular standard or indicator likely to be state-tested that is completely missing from one or more grades (an omission)?

I advise the entire group to be on the alert for these as they listen to each grade-span group's narrative. To illustrate the importance of doing so, I share a story about an elementary school faculty I worked with that had decided to first identify Power Standards in mathematics.

One Faculty's Discovery of a Major Omission

Under the direction of their principal, each grade had met together and followed the Power Standards identification process described above. But they had not yet had the vertical discussions with the grade levels above and below their own. When I returned for my second visit with the faculty at an after-school staff meeting, I asked them to select one particular strand of mathematics that each of their grades could use as a model for building vertical alignment in the other math strands. They decided upon geometry.

I said, "Please list the Power Standards you have selected for geometry at your grade level on a piece of large chart paper. As soon as you are finished, each grade level will post their list in order from kindergarten to grade five and share their process with the rest of us. We will listen and look for any gaps, overlaps, or omissions as the charts go up."

The groups got busy and in a few minutes, I asked the kindergarten teachers to share with the faculty which geometry indicators they had selected and why. They posted their chart on the wall, named the two or three indicators they had selected, and then sat down. The first grade teachers then shared their list of geometry indicators, also short. Things were moving along beautifully!

Now the second grade teachers got up, taped their *blank* chart to the wall, and announced, "We have so many other math indicators in the other math strands that we think are more important than geometry. So we really don't teach geometry that much."

I didn't say anything, nor did the rest of the faculty, and the second grade team sat down. The third grade stood up, echoed the same rationale that the second grade team had offered, and posted their chart. It too was blank.

The fourth grade team could barely contain themselves. They immediately jumped up and posted their chart for all to see. On it were listed several geometry indicators.

They announced, "Do you know how many geometry problems there are on the fourth grade state test? We looked at the released tests from the last two years along with the Testing Information Guide to help us identify which indicators in the geometry strand are most likely to be on the next state test. These are critical for our students to learn if they are going to succeed."

In many states, annual testing is conducted only in certain benchmark years, not in every single grade. In this particular state, the first high stakes test is administered in grade four.

Seeking to ease the tensions in the room, I interjected a question for the entire staff.

"Is the fourth grade test only a fourth grade test, or is it a K-4 test?"

As everyone acknowledged that it was the latter, the fourth grade team said to their colleagues, "There is no way we can teach all the tested geometry concepts and skills in our grade alone. We need all of you in K-3 to introduce and develop essential geometric concepts that we can build upon and extend prior to their taking the state test in fourth grade."

The second and third grade teams immediately realized that if they did not do their part to help their students develop an understanding of geometry concepts listed in the second and third grade indicators, the children would not be ready for fourth grade geometry—and the test scores would reflect that.

Immediately, both of those grade-level groups took down their charts from the wall and opened their math standards to the geometry strand in order to revise their list of Power Standards. The principal beamed, and the rest of the staff applauded. In a few minutes, the revised charts from grades two and three were back up on the wall, and we continued the discussion about vertical alignment.

Grade-span Share Out

The above story's message provides the necessary lens through which to examine the grade-span charts that are now posted on the wall. As each grade-span group takes its turn sharing their lists, the large group focuses on whether the identified standards and indicators build vertically. They are on the lookout for any gaps, overlaps, or omissions.

This is where it is helpful to have the eyes of the entire K-12 group scrutinizing the lists. Sometimes educators in other grade-span teams can be more objective in spotting a need for revision that might otherwise go unnoticed by those who work with those standards each and every day. If any gaps, overlaps, or omissions are noticed by anyone, the team makes note of this for later correction.

When all the grade-span groups finish sharing their lists of proposed Power Standards and have noted any changes they wish to make to close the gaps, remove the overlaps, and eliminate the omissions, I provide the group with the time needed to go back to their tables and *revise both their charts and individual team copies*. They will then have the first draft of their Power Standards for this particular content area section!

But Is This Power Standard Appropriate for My Grade?

Recently an educator voiced concern that although a particular Power Standard was identified in her individual grade level, she did not think it was developmentally appropriate for *all* of her students.

She said to me, "I feel I *have* to teach it, even to those few students who are academically struggling, because this particular standard is not listed in the grade above mine, and I know that it will be important for them to know 'down the road'. It's just beyond what they can *presently* do."

I suggested that she speak with the grade level teachers above her to ask them for help with this situation, saying, "Maybe they would be willing to make sure that it is taught to those individual students when they are more able to grasp it conceptually and demonstrate it skillfully."

These types of discussions may need to take place between educators as part of the Power Standards articulation process so that the standards are not changed, but perhaps the *time* when they are taught for depth of understanding is.

Sequencing the Power Standards

After the grade-span groups make any needed revisions, I call the entire group back together once again.

"There is one additional step you may wish to consider doing at some point before the process is completed. This has to do with scheduling or sequencing the identified Power Standards for instruction and assessment."

I ask the grade-span groups to think about their reporting periods. Whether they follow a quarterly or trimester schedule, *decide which standards should be taught in which individual reporting periods* so that there is a logical progression of when to teach which standards. Math, especially, is hierarchical. Certain concepts and skills must be taught before others if students are to truly understand them. In the same way that school systems develop a scope and sequence for the curricula, a scope and sequence can be determined for the identified Power Standards.

At this point, groups often choose to do a preliminary sequencing of their lists by quarter or trimester. They simply look again at their identified Power Standards and *number them according to which ones need to be taught first, second, and so on*, to promote logical progression of student understanding.

Another Point of View Regarding Sequencing

A middle school science educator in the Midwest recently brought up an excellent point with regard to scheduling the Power Standards by quarter or trimester.

"In science, I continually weave concepts and skills that I taught in an earlier unit into other units. I think it is important for students to see the connections between units of study. To slot certain standards into certain quarters defeats the idea of depth versus breadth and limits me as a science teacher as to when I can teach particular topics. The other problem is that we build our units around our field trips and must schedule our sharing of instructional materials. We need to have the flexibility to teach our units in consideration of all these other factors."

Flexibility, not Restriction

Whether a school or district chooses to sequence the Power Standards by reporting period or not is a matter of local choice and consensus. The essential reason for prioritizing the standards and indicators is to be sure that the most important ones are identified and taught for depth of student understanding. With this shift in emphasis from "coverage to focus," educators find more opportunities to revisit and reemphasize those prioritized standards throughout the year and to help students make standards connections within and between content areas. The broader timeframe of an entire academic school year may better afford educators the flexibility needed to accomplish this.

Power Standards Report Cards

The decision to sequence the Power Standards by quarter or trimester often leads to the revision of district report cards to specify which standards and indicators have been targeted as "essential" and when they will be taught and assessed. Assessments can then be designed for grade levels and content areas that evaluate student understanding of the concepts and skills contained in the Power Standards. These assessments with accompanying scoring guides or rubrics provide the evidence as to what degree of proficiency students have attained relative to the Power Standards and indicators taught in a particular reporting period.

Develop an Action Plan

Whether the same large group needs to meet again to continue the Power Standards identification process for the remaining standards in the same content area or to begin the process in other ones, discussion inevitably turns to the matter of developing an action plan for presenting the information about Power Standards to all educators in the school district. This discussion will also include the need for involving all educators in the selection process.

If the group will not be meeting together again, I encourage participants to brainstorm what their next steps should be in introducing this information to their own schools, departments, or districts. The workshop activities of the day have familiarized participants with the *process*, but now they need to think about how to share that process with their colleagues at their own sites.

The next chapter offers effective methods for implementing this process smoothly in either of the above circumstances. It also discusses the differing roles of the principal, department chair, curriculum coordinator, and central office in developing Power Standards.

Reader's Assignment

Using the process outlined above, develop your own first draft of Power Standards in the content area of your choice. Refer again to the bolded, italicized phrases in this chapter to refresh your memory of the steps in the process. You may also wish to refer to Chapter Eight for a more concise, step-by-step checklist to reference as you work through the entire process.

Appendix D:
Getting Everyone Involved in the Process

> Note: The information in this appendix has been adapted, with permission, from *"Unwrapping" the Standards: A Simple Process to Make Standards Manageable* by Larry Ainsworth.

I remember one elementary educator who, in the first minutes of my workshop, announced in frustration loud enough for all to hear, "So, on top of everything else I have to do, now I have to *'unwrap' the standards!* I just don't have time to do this! Why doesn't the state just hire you to come in and 'unwrap' all of our standards *for* us?"

I looked at the rest of my audience to gauge their reaction to her outcry. Many were nodding in silent agreement.

I thought a moment and answered, "Well, first of all, no one has offered me any money to do this!"

Everyone laughed. The group relaxed. But I had more to say on the subject.

"As logical as your request is, how do you feel when you are just 'handed' a new binder of information—that you had no part in designing—and told to implement it?"

The elementary educator immediately replied, "I don't like it!"

I continued, "Isn't your personal involvement in a process more likely to ensure that you not only understand but will actually *use* the final product in your own classroom?"

"Absolutely," came the answer.

To all the participants I replied, "Then, if you will, let me take you through this 'unwrapping' process today, and when we are finished, I'll ask you for your honest opinions as to whether or not you think this will help improve your instruction and your students' learning. If your answer is 'yes,' then we'll discuss practical ways to 'work smarter, not harder.' Fair enough?"

Everyone agreed, and we got to work. By mid-afternoon, the group had worked through the entire process—including the identification of Big Ideas and Essential Questions. There had been an almost palpable shift in the energy level of participants from when we had started that morning. The educators had become enthusiastic as they began to see the tremendous value and practicality of this process.

How to 'Work Smarter, Not Harder'

The time came to discuss implementation. Without a workable plan that lightened—rather than increased—everyone's workload, I knew that many present would evaluate the workshop positively but not necessarily implement these ideas in their own instructional programs—the true mark of effective professional development.

"Okay, everyone, the moment of truth has arrived. How many of you see value in what we have done today?"

Hands went up all over the room.

"That's great! There's only one snag. What are we going to do about the question asked this morning—the one about how to find the time needed to 'unwrap' all your standards? Would you now like to discuss how to 'work smarter, rather than harder' in this regard?" I asked.

I had everyone's full attention.

"Before I do, let me ask you this. Do you think it is necessary for *every* educator to go through the experience of learning how to 'unwrap' standards *at least once*?"

"Yes!" was the audience response.

I continued, "Once an entire group of educators learns how to 'unwrap' and recognizes firsthand the value of doing so, individuals get together by grade level in elementary and by departments in secondary. They simply divide up the standards and indicators in a selected content area, 'unwrap' the ones they've agreed to do, and share their completed work with colleagues. Many districts are putting their "unwrapped" standards, Big Ideas, and Essential Questions on their websites so everyone in the district can access the work that's been accomplished."

The group could see how this practical way to "work smarter, rather than harder" would indeed lighten their workload instead of adding to it. I went on to give them the specifics as to *how* and *when* this happens.

How *Elementary* Educators Implement These Ideas

Once educators assemble by grade levels at the elementary level to collaboratively
"unwrap," a decision needs to be made. Either target one particular content area or "unwrap" different content areas simultaneously. There are benefits to either approach.

Elementary educators within the same building usually want to "unwrap" all the standards and indicators in one content area, beginning with either language arts or math. The grade-level groups determine a timeframe or schedule for doing this, knowing that the "unwrapping" work will proceed much more quickly the second time because everyone is already familiar with the process. In this way, each selected content area is "unwrapped," one after the other, until all of the work is finished.

The second approach moves the "unwrapping" process along in *more than one* content area at the same time. Groups form according to content areas, and every educator chooses to work in a particular grade level within a specific content area group. Obviously, more time may be needed to "unwrap" several content areas simultaneously if the groups of educators are small and the number of standards and indicators in each content area is large. I recommend that there be at least two educators representing each grade level, if at all possible. The valuable discussion that occurs when two or more grade-level educators collaborate will result in a better quality of "unwrapped" products.

If the group is large, sufficient grade-level representation in each targeted content area will be easier to arrange. The large number of standards and indicators in several content areas can be distributed among the grade-level group members, and the work can be completed in less time.

When arranging district-wide meetings to "unwrap" the elementary standards, content area coordinators typically plan and facilitate the process. Each school sends grade-level and/or content area representatives who collaborate in grade-level teams to "unwrap" the standards. After the work is finished, the collections of "unwrapped" standards with accompanying Big Ideas and Essential Questions are made available to all the elementary educators within the district. But again, I must emphasize the importance of *everyone* first learning the "unwrapping" process before distributing collections of "unwrapped" standards and indicators. Personal experience with this process is a pre-requisite for truly effective implementation.

How *Secondary* Educators Implement These Ideas

Secondary educators invariably organize themselves by content area departments. Within any department, educators are naturally interested in first "unwrapping" the standards for the specific courses they teach. Once each member of the department learns the process, the task of "unwrapping" all the standards and indicators for a particular content area can be accomplished in a relatively short amount of time.

I observed a high school history department chairperson allocate the standards to be "unwrapped" within his department as follows.

He said, "Since I teach the Cold War, I'll 'unwrap' the Cold War standards and indicators. John, you do the ones for your World War II course, and Michelle, you 'unwrap' the U.S. history standards."

He continued on in the same way, asking the remaining members of his department to "unwrap" the particular standards and related indicators they themselves taught. By the end of a few department meetings in which a portion of the time was allocated to "unwrapping," these educators were able to complete the work, including the identification of Big Ideas and Essential Questions.

As each secondary department independently completes the "unwrapping" of its own standards and indicators, the cumulative result will be "unwrapped" standards, Big Ideas, and Essential Questions for every curricular department in the school. These collections can then be posted on the school or district website for easy access and reference by all of its educators.

Suggested Big Ideas and Essential Questions

I advise educators who will be sharing their "unwrapping" work with colleagues to consider adding the adjective "Suggested" in front of the Big Ideas and Essential Questions they write. In this way, individual educators who perhaps identify different Big Ideas and Essential Questions than those of their colleagues can exercise their own judgment in deciding what they should be. When educators review the work of their colleagues, they usually do agree with the Big Ideas and Essential Questions as written, but if not, they have a starting place for determining their own.

A Range of Perspectives

Most educators, once they experience firsthand the "unwrapping" process, see great value in sitting down with colleagues to divide up the standards and indicators and "unwrap" some—but not all—of the standards they personally teach. They then enjoy discussing ways to share their "unwrapping" work, Big Ideas, and Essential Questions in order to prevent everyone from having to "reinvent the wheel."

I appreciated the honesty and candor of the elementary educator described at the beginning of this chapter who did not want to "unwrap" the standards herself, hoping instead that someone else would do the work and then just give it to her. This perspective, however, is more the exception than the rule. Every once in a while an educator expresses a viewpoint that represents the opposite end of the spectrum.

Will Sibley, history teacher at Ben Davis Junior High in Wayne Township, Indianapolis, attended my fall "unwrapping" workshop for his district's secondary educators. When the day concluded, Will expressed a wish to continue "unwrapping" the standards and indicators he personally taught in his history courses. Knowing I was to repeat the workshop the next day for the district's elementary teachers, I suggested to Will and Catherine Cragen, his teaching colleague with whom he had collaborated during the day, that they ask their principal for permission to return the next day to continue their work.

The following day, both Will and Catherine were back! I arranged for them to sit away from the large group so they could collaborate without interruption. When they departed that afternoon, they told me that having that extra day immediately following the initial workshop to continue "unwrapping" enabled them not only to get more of their standards "unwrapped," but that it really "cemented" their understanding of the entire process.

The following spring I conducted a meeting in Wayne Township for teachers from the different schools who had been asked by their principals to assist colleagues within their own buildings as "standards coaches." I was happy to see Will in attendance.

The discussion eventually turned to ways in which we might organize all the teachers in the district to collectively "unwrap" all the K-12 standards in language arts, math, science, and social studies. Will raised his hand to speak.

"I understand that it is time-consuming to 'unwrap' all our standards, and I do agree that it's a good idea to talk about ways to expedite this process district-wide," he said. "But I have to tell you, after 'unwrapping' *all* the standards and indicators I personally teach, it has completely changed my instruction. Because I am now crystal clear about what my students need to learn, I'm teaching better than ever before, and the work the students are producing is far superior to anything I've received in past years. So I just want to go on record as saying that there is great value for teachers to personally do all of their own 'unwrapping.'"

I saw the indisputable wisdom in Will's perspective, one that spoke volumes about what this practice can do for any educator willing to engage fully in the work it requires.

Once "Unwrapped," Forever "Unwrapped"

"Unwrapping" all the standards is certainly going to require an investment of time to accomplish, but the good news is this: Once a standard is "unwrapped," it is "unwrapped" forever. Certainly I do not mean *forever* in the literal sense. If and when the standards are significantly revised at the state or district level, there may indeed be changes in the standards that are substantial enough to warrant a second "unwrapping." But until then, educators and students will benefit from current efforts of educators to "unwrap" all their standards. The work completed now will greatly help educators teach their students the "unwrapped" concepts and skills and guide them to discover the Big Ideas through the standards-based Essential Questions.

But *When* Do Educators Do This?

When implementing any new practice, however valued, the problem is always finding sufficient time to do so when many other matters require attention. Often grade-level teams at the elementary level and department teams at the secondary level "unwrap" their grade-specific standards as the year progresses during their regularly scheduled faculty, grade-level, or department meetings.

To facilitate this at faculty meetings, administrators set the agenda so that business matters can be discussed during the first 20 minutes of an hour meeting, and the remainder of the time can then be used for "unwrapping" standards. In this way, a significant amount of "unwrapping" work can be accomplished in several meetings over the course of a year. This idea of providing educators with job-embedded collaboration time focused on practices to improve instruction and student achievement is becoming increasingly popular.

However, I wish to present another point of view regarding the time issue. If educators can be periodically released from teaching responsibilities for larger blocks of time—half days or even full days—a great deal of "unwrapping" work can be accomplished at higher levels of quality than by parceling out such work at the end of the instructional day when people are tired. I have repeatedly observed the best results in finished "unwrapped" products when educators are mentally fresh, their focus is concentrated and sustained, and they are able to collaborate for longer blocks of time without interruption.

The Spiral Effect

Consider the positive impact on students within a school district if all of its educators from kindergarten through high school made it their regular practice to "unwrap" standards, identify Big Ideas, and pose Essential Questions. With each successive year of schooling, students would be able to build upon a solid foundation of concepts and skills gained the previous year. They would become accustomed to articulating their understanding in terms of Big Ideas and in making connections between new information and what they already know. After several years, the cumulative results in terms of student learning would be dramatic indeed.

By working collaboratively to "unwrap" all the standards, educators are helping each other to utilize more quickly this effective practice in their own instructional programs, thereby moving such an idealistic vision one step closer to reality.

Reader's Assignment

Think about and discuss with colleagues how to implement a systematic plan for "unwrapping" standards, identifying Big Ideas, and writing Essential Questions for one or more content areas in a particular grade or department, in an individual school, or in the entire school district. As you plan for implementation, you may wish to refer to Chapter Nine for a summary checklist of the steps to follow in the entire "unwrapping" standards process.

Index

Norfolk Public Schools 24, 34, 51, 119, 128
norm-referenced assessment 21

O

Ohio 11
oral reading 42
Orange County 34
Oregon 9

P

pacing 29, 136
Palm Springs Unified School District 24
parent involvement 68, 141
PASS 9
pass rate 27
Pearson Learning 41
Pennsylvania 81
performance assessment 6, 24, 28, 34, 36
physical education 30, 44, 124, 127
Pickering, D. 25, 44
portfolio 9
Power Standards 5, 14
power standards 5, 6, 9, 10, 12, 14, 16, 23, 26, 28, 30, 32, 34, 84
pre-school 54
primary standard 24
private schools 122
professional development 63, 135, 173
professional practices 45
Project Zero 116
Pueblo 119

R

reading
  comprehension 43
  programs 41, 43
  skills 41
Reading Research Quarterly 47
Reason to Write 13, 30, 54, 55, 64, 66, 74, 77, 88
Reason to Write Student Handbook 55, 64, 88
Reeves, D.B. 16, 54, 55, 66, 76, 77, 140
Refrigerator Curriculum 142
remedial program 89, 166
report cards 12
research 14, 35, 40, 47, 48, 50, 53, 54, 74, 76, 127, 139
resources 8, 14
Results Fieldbook 120
Right to Learn, The 15, 17, 35, 36, 40, 54, 59, 66, 74, 76, 140
Riverview Gardens 34, 119, 128
rough drafts 69
rubric 24

S

Sanders School 88
Santa Ana 119, 128
SAT 123
Schmoker, M. 120
school improvement plan 120

The Center for Performance Assessment

Mission
The mission of the Center for Performance Assessment is to improve student achievement by building the knowledge and skills of educators and school leaders. We are the world's preeminent source of professional development in the areas of standards, assessment, and accountability.

No Child Left Behind
The Center for Performance Assessment provides seminars, services, and keynote presentations designed to assist your organization in meeting the federal No Child Left Behind Act (NCLB) goals in the areas of instruction, assessment, and accountability. Our interactive seminars are founded on the most recent, scientifically based research and data supporting standards-based education, which is essential to improving student achievement. We guide educators in creating practical methods of instruction and assessment that will significantly improve student achievement and that demonstrate alignment between state standards, instruction, and assessment.

Follow-Up and Implementation
To ensure successful implementation and sustainability of professional development in your organization, we work closely with you to plan follow-up engagements focused specifically on your needs. Because the content of follow-up engagements is driven by your most immediate professional development goals, the possible outcomes are customized. The results of some of our follow-up seminars have included:

- Additional strategies for leaders who must implement new policies and procedures affecting classroom instruction and student achievement
- Additional time for guided practice of new processes and skills
- Additional time for guided collaboration on both lateral and vertical curriculum alignment
- Additional concentrated analysis of seminar content and more strategies for implementation
- Long- and short-term comprehensive professional development plans at the building and district levels
- One-on-one leadership coaching and support
- Small-group focus for teachers and teacher leaders
- Support for new staff members
- Education and support for parents and community members

Our professional development seminars include:
- The Making Standards Work Series, which includes Power Standards, Unwrapping the Standards, and Designing and Developing Performance Assessments
- The Writing Excellence Series, which includes six powerful seminars covering all aspects of classroom writing, from prompts and best practices to modes, genres, and collaborative scoring of student writing

- Effective Teaching Strategies
- Effective Teaching Strategies for Leaders
- Five Easy Steps to a Balanced Math Program
- Student-Generated Rubrics
- Data-Driven Decision Making
- Data-Driven Decision Making for Leaders
- Data Teams
- Accountability in Action
- Accountability System Design
- Daily Disciplines of Leadership
- Assessing Educational Leaders

Resources available from the Center for Performance Assessment

International Performance Assessment System (IPAS):

IPAS is a set of 192 performance assessments, each with at least four tasks and corresponding scoring guides, linked to your state standards. The IPAS assessments can be immediately used in the classroom, or teachers can adapt and expand them to complement established curricula and to meet the specific needs of their students. With IPAS, schools obtain the license to use, reproduce, and modify the assessments without charge or copyright violation.

The performance assessments in the complete IPAS package address state standards in four core subject areas from kindergarten through twelfth grade. The Center will, however, work with you to create an IPAS package custom-fit to the needs of your organization. Your IPAS purchase includes (a) sturdy binders with hardcopies of each performance assessment, and (b) a CD-ROM with electronic copies of each performance assessment for easy uploading to your school's or district's network or intranet. To download and print free sample IPAS assessments, visit www.makingstandardswork.com.

Books:
- *101 Questions & Answers about Standards, Assessment, and Accountability* by Douglas B. Reeves, Ph.D.
- *Accountability for Learning: How Teachers and School Leaders Can Take Charge* by Douglas B. Reeves, Ph.D.
- *Accountability in Action: A Blueprint for Learning Organizations* by Douglas B. Reeves, Ph.D.
- *Assessing Educational Leaders: Evaluating Performance for Improved Individual and Organizational Results* by Douglas B. Reeves, Ph.D.
- *Classroom Instruction That Works: Research-Based Strategies for Increasing Student Achievement* by Robert J. Marzano, Debra J. Pickering, Jane E. Pollock
- *A Handbook for Classroom Instruction That Works* by Robert J. Marzano, Jennifer S. Norford, Diane E. Paynter, Debra J. Pickering, Barbara B. Gaddy

- The Daily Disciplines of Leadership: How To Improve Student Achievement, Staff Motivation, and Personal Organization *by Douglas B. Reeves, Ph.D.*
- *Five Easy Steps to a Balanced Math Program: A Practical Guide for K-8 Classroom Teachers* by Larry Ainsworth and Jan Christinson
- Holistic Accountability: Serving Students, Schools, and Community *by Douglas B. Reeves, Ph.D.*
- *The Leader's Guide to Standards: A Blueprint for Educational Equity and Excellence* by Douglas B. Reeves, Ph.D.
- *Making Standards Work: How to Implement Standards-Based Assessments in the Classroom, School, and District (Third Edition)* by Douglas B. Reeves, Ph.D.
- *Power Standards: Identifying the Standards that Matter the Most* by Larry Ainsworth
- *Performance Assessment Series: Classroom Tips and Tools for Busy Teachers, available in Elementary Edition or Middle School Edition,* by the Center for Performance Assessment
- *Reason to Write: Elementary Edition* by Douglas B. Reeves, Ph.D.
- *Reason to Write Student Handbook: Elementary Edition* by Douglas B. Reeves, Ph.D.
- *Results: The Key to Continuous School Improvement* (Second Edition) by Mike Schmoker, Ph.D.
- *The Results Fieldbook: Practical Strategies from Dramatically Improved Schools* by Mike Schmoker, Ph.D.
- *Student-Generated Rubrics: An Assessment Model to Help All Students Succeed* by Larry Ainsworth and Jan Christinson
- *"Unwrapping" the Standards: A Simple Process to Make Standards Manageable* by Larry Ainsworth
- *What Works in Schools: Translating Research into Action* by Robert J. Marzano

Videos:
- *Accountability for Greater Student Learning* featuring Douglas B. Reeves, Ph.D.
- *Assessments and Scoring Guides Based on Standards, available in Elementary Edition and Secondary Edition*, featuring Douglas B. Reeves, Ph.D.
- *Standards That Work* featuring Douglas B. Reeves, Ph.D.
- KEYNOTE VIDEO: *From the Bell Curve to the Mountain* featuring Douglas B. Reeves, Ph.D. (Includes audio CD)
- KEYNOTE VIDEO: *The Leadership-Learning Connection* featuring Douglas B. Reeves, Ph.D. (Includes audio CD)
- KEYNOTE VIDEO: *Standards Are Not Enough* featuring Douglas B. Reeves, Ph.D. (Includes audio CD)

For more information about our seminars, services, and resources, or to schedule your next professional development event, please contact us.

Toll Free   (800) 844-6599

Phone   (303) 504-9312

Fax   (303) 504-9417

Mail   **Center for Performance Assessment**
                    317 Inverness Way South, Suite 150
                    Englewood, CO 80112

Online   www.makingstandardswork.com

E-mail   resources@makingstandardswork.com

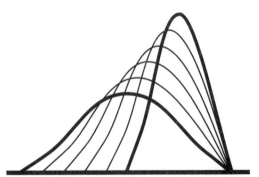

*Improving Student Achievement through
Standards, Assessment, and Accountability*

NOTES

NOTES

NOTES

NOTES

NOTES

NOTES